D0374992

Listening to the Animals

FAITHFUL
GUARDIANS

EDITED BY PHYLLIS HOBE

A GUIDEPOSTS BOOK

Copyright © 2001 by Guideposts, Carmel, New York 10512.
All rights reserved.

No part of this publication may be reproduced, stored in a retrieval system or transmitted, in any form or by any means, electronic, mechanical, photocopying, recording or otherwise without the written permission of the publisher. Inquiries should be addressed to Rights & Permissions Department, Guideposts, 16 East 34th Street, New York, NY 10016.

ACKNOWLEDGMENTS

Every attempt has been made to credit the sources of copyrighted material used in this book. If any such acknowledgment has been inadvertently omitted or miscredited, receipt of such information would be appreciated.

All material that originally appeared in *Guideposts* magazine, *Angels on Earth* or *Daily Guideposts* is reprinted with permission. Copyright © 2000.

"Pud" is from *Running Forward, Looking Back,* by Lynn Seely. Copyright © 2000 by Lynn Seely. "Blind But Brave" and "Lessons in Kitty-Speak," by Lynn Seely, are used by permission of the author.

"Hustler," "No Help in Sight" and "House Calls" are from *The Compassion of Animals,* by Kristin von Kreisler. Copyright © 1997 by Kristin von Kreisler. Published by Prima Publishing.

"Angels of the Sea" is from *True Tales of Animal Heroes,* by Allan Zullo. Copyright © 1998 by The Wordsellers, Inc. Published by Troll Communications L.L.C.

"At the Edge of the Cliff" is from *A Friend Like No Other,* by H. Norman Wright. Copyright © 1999 by H. Norman Wright. Published by Harvest House Publishers.

"A Good Deed Gets a Just Reward" and "Sometimes Angels Come in Disguise," by Renie Szilak Burghardt, are used by permission of the author.

"Mo-tzu," by Myra A. Kosak, is used by permission of the author.

"Zambelli, the Mighty Protector" and "The Cat Who Played Nursemaid," by Carol Wallace, are used by permission of the author.

"Thanks, Blue" and "A Real Lady," by Nancy B. Gibbs, are used by permission of the author.

"Deer Rescue," by Shannon K. Jacobs, is used by permission of the author.

"Search and Rescue," by Ranger Oakes as told to Harry E. Oakes, Jr., and "The Family of Miracle Workers," by Sally A. Voelske, are from *Angel Animals,* by Allen and Linda Anderson. Copyright © 1999 by Allen Anderson and Linda C. Anderson. Published by Plume, a member of Penguin Putnam, Inc.

"Ivan" is from *Shelter Dogs,* by Peg Kehret. Copyright © 1999 by Peg Kehret. Published by Albert Whitman & Company.

"Laddie—Hero and Friend," by Paul Wheeler, is used by permission of the author.

"The Butcher's Kitten," by Bettyanne Gray, is from *Cat Caught My Heart,* by Michael Capuzzo and Teresa Banik Capuzzo. Copyright © 1998 by Michael Capuzzo and Teresa Banik Capuzzo. Published by Bantam Books, a division of Bantam Doubleday Dell Publishing Group, Inc.

"Who's in Charge Here, Anyway?" by Nancy Tomazic, is used by permission of the author.

"Bingo," by Christina Coruth, is used by permission of the author.

(continued on page 208)

Designed by SMS Typography
Illustrations by Michelle Lester
Jacket designed by Dennis Arnold
Printed in the United States of America

Contents

I'LL PROTECT YOU

THIS WAY, PLEASE

I AM HERE

I'LL TAKE CARE OF YOU

You Can Do It

Introduction

*O*ne of the most powerful ways God sends us his love is through his animals. Perhaps he uses them as messengers because they know how to get close to us—or, more likely, he created them for that purpose.

In FAITHFUL GUARDIANS, one of the books in Guideposts' exclusive *LISTENING TO THE ANIMALS* series, we look at some of the many animals who take care of us, sometimes quietly, sometimes dramatically. Whether they comfort us with their abundant love, inspire us to become more than we thought we could be, lift our spirits in the dark times, help us to carry our burdens or protect us from harm, they assure us that God cares deeply about each and every one of us. The true stories in this book tell us that God is always near.

In *I'll Protect You,* our first chapter, we meet some remarkable animals who come between us and danger. There is Pud, a lovable mutt who went running with his owner every morning and saved the man's life when he was attacked by a vicious dog. In "Angels of the Sea," Allan Zullo tells us about a young girl named Calisa who was befriended and protected by a family of dolphins—just as a shark was closing in on her. Shannon K. Jacobs writes about a herd of mule deer who led rescuers to a man who was badly hurt when he fell off his horse.

The stories in *This Way, Please,* bring us animals who help us to find our way when we are lost. Ivan, a dog who became a hearing-aide for a young deaf woman, led her little daughter to safety when their house caught fire. Christina Coruth recalls her childhood companion, Bingo, whose incessant barking annoyed her family until the day he saved Christina from two suspicious-looking men. "Sometimes Angels Come in Disguise" is Renie Szilak Burghardt's delightful story about a doe who led her home when she got lost in the woods.

Our third chapter, *I Am Here,* brings us stories about the many animals who bring us comfort in our anxious moments. You will be touched by Micki Siegel's description of the therapy animals who visited the children who survived the Oklahoma City bombing and were able to communicate love and reassurance when no one else could get through to them. "The Cat Who Played Nursemaid" is Carol Wallace's tribute to a devoted cat who lost his dearest animal friend to leukemia. Veterinarian Lillian M. Roberts discovers that pets come in all shapes, sizes—and species—when an anxious father and child bring in their sick rat, and she goes all-out to save him.

The stories in *I'll Take Care of You* are about the animals who sense our needs and go to extraordinary lengths to help us. Anne Watkins writes about Coco, her miniature poodle, who comforted her and then went for help when she collapsed and was going into a diabetic coma. In "Betty Boop and the Gang," Philip Gonzalez' cat-loving dog, Ginny, rescues a lame, wild kitten who becomes a loving, ministering nursemaid to Philip and his growing family of adopted strays. Thirza Peevey introduces us to Greta, a scrawny, abused pony who grew into a beautiful, healthy horse and repaid Thirza for her loving care by saving her life.

In our final chapter, *You Can Do It,* you'll meet some of the animals who refuse to let us take No for an answer. When John M. Alston, who lost both his legs in Korea, adopts a needy dog to be his companion, he has no idea that his new friend will insist that he learn to walk again. In "Charlie, the Arctic Explorer," Karen Derrico introduces us to a dog who accompanies his owner, Helen Thayer, on her solo expedition to the North Pole. Lynn Seely, a runner recovering from back surgery, began to think her running days were over—until she realized that her cat, Mesha, had other ideas.

How very often an animal has made a difference in our lives, and in the directions we take. And how incredible that they seem to be there at the exact moment we need them. We don't even have to ask for their care and help. They just know. And they just give. With their abundant love and trust, we can do anything. Perhaps God had that in mind all along when he sent them our way.

PHYLLIS HOBE

FAITHFUL
GUARDIANS

I'll Protect You

"He is not far from each one of us."

ACTS 17:27, KJV

$\mathcal{S}$tep outside at night, all by yourself. Scary, isn't it? Even the streetlights don't help. But step outside to walk your dog and say hello to a passing neighbor, and you don't even think about it. Whether your way is light or dark, it makes no difference when you're in the company of someone who cares about you. You're at home in the world.

Pud

LYNN SEELY

The weather was really perfect for this race. The distance of the course was a 5-K, which means each runner goes a distance of five kilometers, or a little over three miles. Clear blue skies and cool temperatures made it perfect for running.

As I stepped up to the starting line, I noticed a man who was wearing an unusual belt with a metal ring attached to it. A leash was fastened to the ring. A dog was sitting quietly at the end of the leash. He was a drab swirl of brown and black fur, with a head that appeared too large for his body. This dog had a huge scar across the right side of his face. The scar ran from his ear down into the upper lip and caused the lip to curl up, exposing a few crooked teeth.

It was probably one of the ugliest dogs I'd ever seen in my life, but I had to admit he seemed to be well behaved. My curiosity drew me a few feet closer to them.

The dog was not staring at the milling, noisy crowd of runners. Instead, he gazed intently at his master's face. There seemed to be an unusual intelligence in those dark brown eyes. I overheard the owner of the dog mention that Pud (which rhymes with *good*) was a great companion. He added that it was good to have Pud by his side again.

"Well, Vic," the other runner replied, "it's just amazing that he survived that terrible attack. What a dog!" The runner then reached over and gave Pud a friendly pat on the top of his head. The dog seemed to enjoy the attention.

At this point, the race official announced that the race was about to start and a few moments later the starter's gun went off. All runners started the race with enthusiasm. This was a flat course and the weather was quite cool. Most of us would enjoy the race today.

After a few minutes of running, I saw the man and his dog ahead of me. I increased my pace a little so I could run closer to them. The dog, as well as the conversation I overheard just before the race started, intrigued me.

The dog was running just slightly in front of the man, but was not pulling on the leash. I ran alongside the man for a few minutes and we exchanged names. He told me his name was Vic and he was celebrating his sixty-sixth birthday that day. "New age group," he added, smiling.

After a short time I picked up my pace as planned and slowly moved ahead. I didn't see Vic and his dog again until after the race was over. Vic walked up to me and asked how I had liked the race, then he leaned down and gave his dog a friendly pat on the head.

"Fine," I replied. "And how about the two of you?" I said, referring to Vic and his four-legged friend. "Oh, we did just grand today," he said with a big grin.

I was curious to find out more about the dog. I asked Vic, "How did he get the name Pud?" Vic told me Pud's full name was Pudding Pie. "That is a story in itself," he explained. "According to his former owner," Vic winked at Pud and tugged affectionately on the dog's ear, "Pud had a great affection for any type of pudding, any kind at all. As a young puppy he could smell it being cooked and came racing into the kitchen as soon as some was being prepared. There he would sit with wagging tail, happily anticipating a spoonful of the delicious substance. His litter mates never seemed to notice the pudding but Pud was unfailing in his devotion to get this treat. His tail never wagged so vigorously while other food was prepared, so his first owner thought that Pudding Pie was the perfect name for the small dark puppy."

Vic concluded, "The name stuck, although when I acquired him, I did shorten it a bit to Pud."

Vic, Pud and I headed over to some tables and chairs that had been set up under some trees as we waited for the race results to be announced. Vic turned to me and asked, "Did you notice the large scar across Pud's face?" I confirmed that I had noticed it and said I had wondered how it happened. "It's quite a story of Pud's courage, and I'll be happy to tell you all about it as soon as I give him some water."

Vic was about to tell me the most amazing story of Pud's courage and how this 40-pound dog of questionable parentage had protected him. Pudding Pie was sprawled in the shade of a tree where we were sitting. Vic poured out some water into a paper dish and Pud lapped it up without getting to his feet. I studied Pud's face as he drank. The scar that ran from the ear to the upper lip was still painful looking. It was healed, but it seemed to cover a wound that had been done recently.

He had probably never been an attractive dog, due to the murky colors of black and brown and also due to the fact that his head was too large for the size of his body. Yet the more I studied him, the more I was drawn in by the gentle, intelligent expression in his eyes. He was gazing around at the crowd, watching carefully, but every few moments his face turned toward his owner, Vic. I could tell Pud was monitoring his master. If he sensed Vic was okay, then all was well with the world.

Vic began his story of how Pud had come to be disfigured. Some weeks earlier Vic had decided to change his running route. He picked an area where he had not been before but he had been told about. His new route would go through a residential neighborhood for approximately one mile, then up a small hill to a wooded area. Vic had been told that this wooded area was an ideal spot for runners and that a two-mile trail was well marked. It was an oval circuit and would return him to his starting point at the edge of the neighborhood.

"One morning about six o'clock, we got ready to go on a run. As usual, Pud was all tail-wags and toothy-grins at the thought of going on his daily run with me." Vic rubbed Pud's head, then he continued, "We headed out the door toward the new route and slowly started to run. I always had Pud by my side on these daily runs. It was a great comfort to me to have my buddy along. Little did I know how much Pud was about to do for me."

As Vic and Pud neared the residential area, both of them were thoroughly enjoying the run. Nothing was out of place on that pleasant morning. After passing through the neighborhood, they started up a small hill. The pace slowed as dog and man accommodated for the incline.

"Pud always runs a few steps in front of me, off to one side slightly." Vic pointed to the device he had with him and explained, "I use this special belt that the leash attaches to. I never have to worry about Pud jerking me because I have trained him to run without pulling. As we neared the woods that morning, I decided to take the leash off. Pud always obeys me and stays close, even when off the leash."

Just after they topped the small hill, they entered the woods where the trail began. "Immediately after entering the woodland area," Vic said, "a huge black form burst out onto the trail and blocked our path. Startled, Pud and I stopped instantly! There, in front of us, with his head lowered, hackles raised, and growling menacingly, stood the largest, meanest dog I had ever seen. Its eyes had an unnatural quality to them, almost evil. The dog was actually frothing at the mouth as he growled and showed his fangs."

All three stood without moving for a few seconds. The large dog took no notice of Pud, who was not moving or making a sound. Suddenly, the animal started walking, stiff-legged, toward Vic. For a brief moment Vic wondered if he could outrun the dog, or maybe make it to a tree.

Vic's voice wavered with emotion as he said, "Before I could turn and run, the huge dog lunged at me, aiming for my throat, growling like some demon from hell! But that dog had forgotten Pud! The instant the monster lunged toward my throat, Pud reacted fearlessly."

Less than half the size of the attacking menace, faithful Pud leaped through the air and crashed into the attacking dog, knocking him over. Pud began snarling and fighting with all his might in order to save Vic.

Tears brimmed in Vic's eyes as he reached over and rubbed Pud's head. Then he resumed his story. "Because of Pud, I was able to escape to a safe distance away from the dog. I then turned and called Pud to me."

The dust had been stirred up and the dogs were fighting so intensely that Vic couldn't tell what was happening. Poor Pud was unable to escape. Never had Pud been in a fight and this dog was more than twice Pud's size!

Vic continued, "I glanced around frantically for something to use as a weapon and saw a limb that had fallen from a tree. I grabbed it and went racing back to the tangle of those two fighting dogs. I knew my little buddy was in a fight for his life. I was screaming like a madman and began hitting the attacker. The dog finally had enough! He ran away with his tail between his legs. I dropped my stick and knelt over Pud, my poor, dear friend. I was so worried he might die. It looked bad."

Pud was panting hard and blood was pouring down his face from a terrible wound, yet he still managed to wag his tail slightly as Vic caressed him.

"I quickly took off my shirt and wrapped it around Pud's head," he said. "Then I gently lifted my buddy up and quickly carried him to the nearest house where I begged for a ride to my home. Fortunately for Pud, the people were happy to help.

"As soon as I reached my house, I placed Pud in my car on the front seat next to me, then rushed him to the nearest animal hospital. He never whimpered or barked on the drive, he just lay very still. I was so worried he would go into shock and die!

"The veterinarian spent quite a long time working over Pud, and as you can see, Pud recovered. The vet asked if Pud's rabies shots were up to date. They were, thank goodness. The vet did mention that had Pud not acted as he had, I might have had to undergo painful rabies shots. That is, had I survived the attack!"

Vic sat there, his face beaming with pride as he added, "Little Pud had placed his life in danger to save me from possible death or, at the least, great injury.

As Vic praised Pud, the dog gazed into his owner's face with what I can only describe as pure joy. Pud had not run away, yet clearly he could have, or Pud could have simply barked while the vicious animal attacked Vic. If Vic had been attacked, he would have been seriously injured, or worse. There had only been a brief moment for little Pud to decide if he would run away, bark, or attack the huge snarling dog. He proved his devotion and bravery in one instant!

I'd be proud to have a dog just like Pudding Pie. He is quite a dog! In fact, I think he is a wonder!

from RUNNING FORWARD, LOOKING BACK

Hustler

KRISTIN VON KREISLER

$\mathcal{D}$ebbie Inions rode out early one evening on her quarter horse, Pat, to check the cattle on her farm in Alberta, Canada. As the sky darkened over the farm's 2,100 acres, she took a shortcut through some brush. Hustler, her German shepherd, bounded through the grass beside her.

As they headed up a hill, a sudden rustling in the bushes startled Pat. He shied, jumped, and brushed against a fence. Since he couldn't run through it, he whirled around and shied again. Debbie, thrown off-balance, fell to the ground. Her leg was shattered. Blood poured from the wound where a broken bone had torn through her skin.

She lay crumpled on the steep hill. Everything seemed blurred; overwhelming pain throbbed through her body. Hustler rushed over and sniffed her as if he wanted to help, but she needed more than he could offer. She needed a doctor as quickly as she could get to one.

But no one would find her, she feared, for many hours. Her children were home, asleep, and would not miss her. Her husband, Brian, was out seeding barley; he probably wouldn't come home and see that she was gone until well after midnight. Even when he *did* begin searching, it might be morning by the time he found her. Why would he even think of looking in the middle of the brush a quarter of a mile from the nearest road?

With Hustler beside her, Debbie tried to push her pain to the back of her mind, so she could concentrate on what to do. Maybe if she could get Pat to go home, someone would see him walking along with an empty saddle and know that she was in trouble. But when she swished a stick at him, he took off through the bush, in a direction where no one would ever see him.

Crestfallen, Debbie told herself that she'd have to get up and walk home on her own, no matter how bad the pain was. But each time she tried to move, her broken bones scraped together, causing more waves of excruciating pain. After she tried to stand three times, the agony was so overwhelming that she thought she'd faint. Exhausted, she lay down beside Hustler. He moved closer, and his furry body kept her warm.

Hustler had proved to be an exceptional dog, a rare combination of aggression and sensitivity. With the energy of three ranch hands, he herded cattle. He nipped at their legs to keep them moving and loaded them onto chutes. But he was also extremely gentle. Hustler's breeder had told Debbie that the dog had once picked up a baby bird who had fallen from its nest. Hustler carried the bird in his mouth to the breeder and had seemed concerned about the tiny fledgling.

Knowing Hustler's capacity for compassion, Debbie was shocked when he abruptly pricked his ears, stood up, and shot down the hill. How could he be so *un*concerned about her? How could he possibly amuse himself chasing deer when she was so badly hurt? Especially when, at any moment, she might go into shock or bleed to death?

He returned, stood over her, bared his teeth, and growled

into the darkness. She'd never seen him look so fierce. Squinting to figure out just what he was growling at, Debbie saw two coyotes only fifteen feet away. They curled their lips and growled back at Hustler. Creeping closer, their paws crunched on leaves and underbrush.

Debbie cringed, the back of her neck prickling with terror. Coyotes rarely approached a person unless they felt threatened. Perhaps she was close to their den and was upsetting them. Whatever their problem, these two could easily attack her, she believed. For protection, she leaned closer to Hustler. He snarled, leaped over her, and chased the coyotes back into the brush again.

Debbie heard thrashing, barking, angry snapping, and pained yipping. The darkness and thick brush prevented her from seeing who was winning the fight. She lay there, faint and queasy, not knowing whether Hustler or the coyotes would emerge from the brush.

When Hustler finally returned, Debbie was immensely grateful. Once again, the dog switched from fierce aggression to pure kindness. He lay down beside her, apparently trying to warm her, and gently licked and cleaned her bloody leg.

Every few minutes, throughout the night, the coyotes would circle around her. She kept screaming at them to scare them off, and each time Hustler chased them back into the bush. Debbie listened to the snarling and the snapping of every encounter. Gripped by fear, she waited to see whether Hustler would win. Each time he returned. But the odds were against him, two to one, and she wasn't sure how long he could last, no matter how much he wanted to protect her.

The coyotes howled, and rain started to fall. The wind picked up. Debbie began trembling so violently from cold and shock that the shaking hurt her leg. She was afraid she'd pass out from the pain.

"Get a grip, Deb," she kept repeating.

She had to stay conscious in order to defend herself. And Hustler also had to stay alert. She hung on to him, *willing* him not to relax his vigil. He pressed against her as if to reassure her that he was there.

About 1:30 that morning, Brian came home from the barley fields and found all the windows open. He was immediately concerned: Debbie always closed them in the evening. When he also discovered that her horse and riding boots were missing, his concern escalated to anxiety. He rushed to his daughter's room and shook her awake.

"Where's your mother?"

"She went to check the cows."

Brian told himself not to worry; he would find her. Yet his body tensed as he ran to his all-terrain vehicle and started combing the farm for Debbie. About 4 A.M., Brian caught sight of Hustler in the car's headlights. The German shepherd was chasing two coyotes through a clearing. Debbie had to be close by.

Brian turned off the motor and ran after Hustler. "Debbie? Debbie!" he called through the wind.

She heard him but was so weak and hoarse that she could barely whisper. Straining to listen, Brian finally heard her answer. Then Hustler appeared and led Brian to her.

"Thank God, you found me!" Debbie moaned.

Her pain was so intense that Brian dared not try to move her. He would have to go for help. As he sped away, Debbie looked around, afraid again. Where was Hustler? The dog was gone. Perhaps he'd followed Brian home and left her all alone.

But she never should have doubted his devotion to her. When the coyotes resumed their howling in the brush, Hustler returned and crouched beside her head. Each time the coyotes drew close, he chased them off, as he'd managed to do for nearly seven hours. After each fight, he curled up protectively beside her.

Brian left a flashlight on the road to signal the paramedics and rushed back to Debbie with blankets. Just before dawn, the ambulance arrived. Paramedics loaded Debbie onto a stretcher, then into the ambulance. The coyotes watched, panting, from less than forty feet away.

For the next two weeks, Debbie recuperated in the hospital. Hustler waited at home and refused to eat. Whenever Brian returned from visiting her, Hustler raced to the truck and peered inside. Each time he saw that she wasn't there, his eyes looked sad and troubled.

Debbie finally did come home. She opened the truck door; and before she could climb out, Hustler, ecstatic, jumped up to rest his feet on the running board. He seemed to sense how fragile she was, and instead of pushing against her for affection, he carefully sniffed her broken leg from toe to hip.

Through four surgeries the following year, Debbie slowly graduated from a wheelchair to a walker to crutches to a cane. No matter what method she used to get around, Hustler followed her every move and guarded her. When Debbie was finally well enough to ride Pat again to check the cattle, Hustler was her ever-present guard, a graceful silhouette crossing the fields in the moonlight.

from THE COMPASSION OF ANIMALS

Angels of the Sea

ALLAN ZULLO

Calisa Mills's heart pounded with excitement and goose-bumps rippled her arms. She was so nervous she was afraid she wouldn't be able to breathe through her snorkel.

The eighth-grader from New Jersey was about to realize a lifelong dream—swimming with dolphins. She and her family were on vacation off the northeast coast of Australia. They had hired Captain Joe Baker and his weathered wooden boat to take them to an area several miles offshore where people-friendly dolphins frolicked.

Captain Baker cut the engine. "This is the spot," he announced to Calisa, her fifteen-year-old brother, Brooks, and their parents, Don and Karen. The captain's instructions were simple: "Don't touch the dolphins. If they want to, they will touch you. Swim with your hands at your sides and don't swim directly at them or behind them. If you do, they might think you're about to attack. Try to make eye contact and show them you want to be their friend. Finally, have fun!"

Calisa inhaled through her nose, sucking the mask tightly against her tanned face. She bit down on the mouthpiece of her snorkel and slid off the boat into the shimmering, crystal-clear water.

Within seconds, Calisa heard the wondrous clicks and

whirs of the dolphins, but she couldn't see them. Suddenly, a flash of gray and white zipped beneath her. It was a ten-foot-long (3-m) adult dolphin.

As instructed, Calisa dove down and made eye contact with the sleek mammal. She smiled through her face mask and tried her best to send a mental message. *Hi. I'm really happy to meet you. I think you are the most beautiful, most awesome animal in the world. I hope you like me. I want to be your friend.*

As Calisa met the dolphin's steady gaze, she felt he actually understood what she was thinking. His lovable eyes shone with an intelligence she had seen in no other animal.

In her excitement, Calisa forgot that her lungs were screaming for air. *I don't want to leave you, but I've got to get some air. Don't go away. I'll be right back.*

When she broke the surface, Calisa joyfully shouted, "This is so awesome! I can't believe it!"

From the stern of the boat, Captain Baker chuckled. "Enjoy, my young friend. Enjoy these angels of the sea."

Before Calisa had a chance to head down again, two dolphins streaked by her, one on each side, leaving a stream of bubbles in their wake. With her hands by her side, she kicked hard, but the dolphins moved too fast for her to keep up.

They made a U-turn and swam so close to Calisa that she was convinced they would bump into her. *I want to touch them so badly. They seem to like me. Maybe if I pretend to touch them accidentally, they won't mind.* But the moment that thought came into her head, the dolphins sped away. *They can read my mind!* Calisa thought.

Calisa was alone for only a minute before a mother dolphin and her calf circled the enchanted girl. The mother stopped, poked her head out of the water, and stared at her. Treading water, Calisa took off her mask so that the dolphin could get a good look at her. Then the calf stuck his head out too.

"Hi, guys! Nice to meet you. My name is Calisa."

The calf squeaked and shook his head before submerging. His mother joined him and the two began swimming slowly away. Calisa put on her mask, adjusted her snorkel and slipped under the water.

Suddenly, Calisa felt a strange jolt, almost like a mild electrical shock. It startled her so much that she stopped swimming and returned to the surface, bewildered by the odd sensation.

The mother dolphin surfaced, too, and opened her mouth, exposing dozens of cone-shaped teeth in a dolphin smile. Then she and her calf swam off.

Back on the boat, the elated Mills family breathlessly shared their dolphin experiences with each other. When Calisa mentioned that she'd felt a slight electrical shock, the captain applauded. "Ah, you're so fortunate. The mother dolphin echolocated you."

"What's that mean?" she asked.

"The dolphin uses sonar to scan the water. This sonar is incredibly precise. In fact, a dolphin can echo-locate a shark a half mile (.8 k) away and determine whether its stomach is full or empty. If the shark's stomach is empty . . . " Joe stopped, hoping one of the Millses would finish the sentence.

" . . . then the dolphin better stay away from the shark," said Brooks, "because the shark could be hungry, right?"

"Very good!" the captain said. "Calisa, the mother dolphin sent out a sonar signal. That's what you felt. She must have found something quite interesting about you."

"Yeah," Brooks piped up, "the dolphin probably never saw such a weird-looking human before!"

He laughed and then ducked when Calisa flung her mask at him. "Not even your dumb remark is going to ruin this day," she said.

The old wooden boat was chugging back to port when an agitated dolphin began crisscrossing in front of the bow. Several times he swam under the boat and then came up on the other side, squeaking loudly.

Captain Baker stepped away from the wheel and peered over the side. "I'm not sure why he's doing that. Maybe he wants us to follow him. It's not uncommon for a dolphin to guide ships. Let me tell you about Pelorus Jack. He was one of the most famous dolphins ever because he saved an untold number of lives.

"Pelorus Jack lived many years ago, long before ships had the sophisticated electronic gear they use today. He was named after the pelorus, a device used for navigation.

"This amazing dolphin lived in the waters off New Zealand in a channel known as French Pass. This channel is extremely hazardous because it's full of rocks and has very strong currents. Why, I can't tell you how many ships have been wrecked in French Pass—hundreds, maybe thousands. But no ship was ever wrecked when Pelorus Jack was at work."

Joe stroked his bushy red beard. "Is that dolphin still in front of us?"

"Yes," said Brooks. "I hope we don't run over him."

"Ah, mate, there's no chance of that. Now, on with my story. PJ—that's what I call Pelorus Jack—was first seen by the sailors of the Boston schooner called the *Brindle*. As the ship entered French Pass, PJ appeared at the bow just like that dolphin is doing right now. One of the crewmen got out a gun. He wanted to shoot the dolphin.

"Fortunately, the captain's wife gave the sailor a tongue-lashing and he put away his gun. PJ then guided the ship through that narrow channel with no problem. For years thereafter, PJ safely led many other ships through French Pass.

"He was so dependable that when ships reached French Pass, the sailors would look for him. If they didn't see him, the ship would circle outside the channel and wait for him to show up. That's how good he was.

"One day, a ship named the *Penguin* entered French Pass. A stupid passenger pulled out a gun and shot PJ. The dolphin was bleeding badly and swam off. The crew was so furious, they nearly lynched the passenger. Fortunately, the *Penguin* managed to make it safely through French Pass without PJ's help.

"No one saw PJ for several weeks, and the sailors assumed that he had died. Other ships had to navigate through the treacherous waters without his help. But one day, PJ showed up and began guiding ships again. He had recovered and was willing to forgive the humans—most of them.

"You see, the next time the *Penguin* entered French Pass, PJ disappeared under the water. The ship had to manage on its own. For several more years, PJ helped other ships get through the channel, but he never would guide the *Penguin*. Finally, the ship was wrecked on some shoals in French Pass and sank, taking dozens of passengers and crewmen to their deaths."

Calisa leaned over the bow to watch the dolphin. He continued to jump in front of the boat, squeaking and shaking his head. "Captain," she asked, "do you think this dolphin is trying to tell us something?"

Joe walked over to the bow and pondered the scene. "It seems like he wants us to stop this boat," he said.

After the captain cut off the engine, the dolphin crisscrossed the bow, stuck his head out of the water, squeaked, and snorted through his blow hole. "I better take a look under the boat," said Joe. He fitted himself with a snorkel, mask, and fins and jumped in.

Captain Baker examined the bow while the dolphin circled nearby. After several minutes, Joe climbed aboard and said, "Would you believe that dolphin was warning us of a problem?"

"What is it?" asked Calisa's father.

"There's a crack in the bow. It needs my quick attention or else we'll all be taking an unscheduled—and quite long—swim." The captain went below deck and saw water leaking through the crack. He cranked up a pump to suck out the water and smeared the crack from the inside with a special repair plaster. "That'll hold until we get back to the marina," he declared. "No need to worry."

"Did the dolphin save us from sinking?" Brooks asked.

"That's quite possible, son."

Calisa scanned the horizon, looking for the dolphin, but he had left. "We didn't even get to say thank you. I can't wait to get back home and tell everyone that we were saved by a dolphin."

She soon would have an even better—and more terrifying—story to tell.

Two days after the Millses swam with the dolphins, they chartered a forty-foot (12-m) yacht for a weekend of exploring along the Great Barrier Reef. The Reef is the largest coral formation in the world, stretching more than 1,250 (2,012 km) off the Australian state of Queensland.

The yacht, skippered by Calisa's father, soon came upon a pod of about twenty dolphins. "Are they rounding up a school of fish?" Brooks wondered out loud.

"No, I think they're racing toward the boat to greet us!" Calisa replied excitedly.

The dolphins swam alongside the sailboat, body-surfing the waves as the Mills family whooped and hollered. Occasionally, one of the dolphins would swim on its side and gaze at them in a friendly way. "Daddy, can we please stop and swim with the dolphins?" Calisa begged.

Her father eyed the sky, which was rapidly darkening with threatening clouds. "We can't stop here. We need to get to a protected area before this storm hits." Within the hour, they had anchored in a bay ringed on three sides by coral shoals. The storm soon hit, rocking the sailboat with strong gusts and heavy rain.

The next morning dawned quiet and clear. Calisa, the first to rise, walked onto the deck and admired the pinkish glow of the sky. The only sound was the water lapping against the hull. Then her ears detected a faint but distinctive clicking sound. Calisa scurried to the side. Dancing in the water was a young bottlenose dolphin no bigger than she was.

"Hi, sugar!" shouted Calisa. "How are you this morning?"

The little dolphin circled once, then leaped out of the water, returning so perfectly that he hardly made a splash. *I've got to go in,* thought Calisa. *I can't pass up another chance to swim with a dolphin.*

Not even bothering to change into a swimsuit, Calisa quickly grabbed her snorkel, fins, and mask out of the storage box. In her haste, she gashed her arm on the edge of the lid. As her arm started to bleed, she thought, *I don't want to waste any more time. The salt water will wash out the cut.* She jumped overboard.

The dolphin came right toward Calisa, then dipped down.

The girl dove after him. Once again, she felt the zapping sensation of echo-location. *Do you like me as much as I like you?* Calisa wondered.

The dolphin moved closer and turned his back to her, waving the dorsal fin on his back. *Do you want me to touch you?* Up to now, Calisa had been careful not to get too close to him. But the dolphin made it clear he wanted her to grab on to his fin. As soon as she did, he took off with Calisa holding on for dear life.

The dolphin dove down about ten feet (3 m), then returned to the surface, allowing Calisa to catch her breath before they went for another underwater ride. *I'm riding on the back of a dolphin!* Calisa marveled. *What a dream—only it's real!*

But the dreamy moment was about to turn horrifying.

The dolphin picked up speed, slipping under the surface and heading out toward the open water. As he dove deeper than before, Calisa's enjoyment turned to concern. *I can't go any farther with you. We're too far away from the boat. Besides, I need air.* She let go and drifted to the surface while the dolphin disappeared.

Calisa realized that she was alone in the water, about a quarter mile (.4 km)—more than the length of four football fields—from the boat. Her arm ached, and she noticed that her gash was deeper than she had thought and still bleeding. But she didn't care. Her mind and heart brimmed with affection and gratitude for her blissful, unforgettable encounter with the little dolphin. Calisa lazily backstroked toward the boat.

Five minutes later, as she rolled over onto her stomach to do the breast stroke, she spotted a dorsal fin. *Oh, good. He came back.* Then Calisa looked more closely and her body tensed with fright. *That's not a dolphin. It's a shark!*

She whirled around, hoping to see an exposed rock that she could reach before the shark came any closer. But the nearest rock was on the other side of the boat.

"Help!" Calisa yelled. "Dad! Mom! Brooks! Shark!" She began to shake in terror as the shark, smelling the blood from her cut arm, zeroed in on his prey. *I'm going to get eaten alive!*

Calisa had never felt so alone, so helpless. She screamed for help until her throat burned. But her family continued to sleep soundly below deck. The shark circled Calisa slowly, as if he wanted to torture her before he bit into her flesh. Then the fiendish creature tightened the circle and closed in for the kill.

I'm going to die. I hope it's quick. Resigned to her fate, Calisa watched as the shark started his final, death-dealing charge.

Calisa curled up in a ball, closed her eyes, and sucked in a deep breath, thinking it would be the last one she ever took. Floating in the calm water, she waited for the shark's razor-sharp teeth to rip into her trembling body. After several agonizing seconds, she heard a thud and a splash. But she was afraid to open her eyes. She didn't want the last picture in her mind to be the open mouth of a killer shark.

Then she heard beautiful sounds that gave her hope—dolphins clicking, whirring, and squealing. Calisa straightened up and stuck her head out of the water. She was stunned by what she saw.

Five yards (4.6 m) away from her, two adult dolphins were taking turns slamming into the side of the shark. With each blow, the shark thrashed in the water and backed away. When he tried to swim toward Calisa, the dolphins darted in front of him and wouldn't let him pass.

Moments later, two more dolphins appeared and rammed into the shark. He tried to bite them, but they were much too quick. Meanwhile, the little dolphin that had given Calisa a ride swam in a tight, protective circle around her.

By now, the battered shark had endured enough head butting from the dolphins. He turned and swam away.

Calisa bobbed in the water, overwhelmed by the drama that had unfolded in front of her. When she realized that the dolphins had saved her from a horrible death, she sobbed with relief.

The little dolphin hovered close to her, clicking and spewing water through his blow hole. "Oh, thank you," Calisa said, stroking his back. "Now I see what you were trying to do earlier. You knew there was a hungry shark between me and the boat, and you were trying to get me away from him. When I let go and started swimming toward the boat, you knew I wouldn't make it back without getting attacked, so you went and got help, didn't you? You dolphins really are the angels of the sea!"

from TRUE TALES OF ANIMAL HEROES

At the Edge of the Cliff

H. NORMAN WRIGHT

Woodie, a collie mix from Cleveland, Ohio, saved his mistress' fiancé from drowning. Rae Ann and her fiancé, Ray, were walking in a forest preserve near a river when Ray said he'd like to take a good picture of the river. He asked Rae Ann to hold Woodie while he searched out the proper vantage point, but a few minutes later Woodie began to pull away from Rae Ann. The dog finally broke loose and ran off in the direction Ray had gone. Rae Ann ran after him. When she reached the dog on the top of a nearby cliff, she saw Ray lying at the bottom of the cliff, eighty feet below, face down in the shallow river. Woodie jumped off the cliff and pulled Ray's face out of the water. By the time Rae Ann reached the river, help had arrived. Woodie had broken his hip in his leap off the cliff. Ray was also badly injured, but he was alive, thanks to Woodie's courage.

from A FRIEND LIKE NO OTHER

A Good Deed Gets a Just Reward

RENIE SZILAK BURGHARDT

As the beautiful Current River winds its way through Ripley County, Missouri, it sings its sometimes tumultuous, sometimes placid song. The blue-green waters of the river are home to many species of fish, and on its banks and in the sky above it, wildlife thrives.

Should one be fishing on the river in the fall of the year, one is likely to see an Osprey dive in, just ahead, and come up with a fish in his talons. The Great Blue Heron is a patron of the river year-round, and Bald Eagles soar the skies here in the winter.

People from all across the country come to enjoy the Current River. Fishing, boating, swimming, camping and inner tubing are popular activities. But my favorite thing to do on the river is to go out on a boat, courtesy of a son, drive up several miles, shut the motor off, and allow the currents of the river to carry us back at a leisurely pace. It is a totally relaxing floating experience, with much to see and ruminate upon. Gazing down into the clear water, I'm likely to see a river bass swim by. Gazing into the sky, a Red-Tailed Hawk might be soaring gracefully. And on the shores, I have seen a wild turkey hen having a drink with her turkey chicks. Beauty, serenity, and cool breezes make for a most pleasant experience on these excursions.

Sometimes, though, a boat ride may net an unexpected surprise. Such as the one I had on a lovely fall day, five years ago. Greg had just shut the motor off, and I leaned back and let one of my feet dangle in the water. The trees on the bluffs above the river were dressed in their fall finery, the sky was exceptionally blue, and some turtles were taking a sunbath on a fallen tree branch nearby. Suddenly, the peace and tranquillity of the moment were interrupted by the piercing, pitiful cries of an animal.

"Greg, some animal is in distress up ahead. Let's go see what it is," I immediately said. Of course, Greg, having inherited a soft spot for helpless animals from his mom, did exactly what I asked.

"Look, there's something on that gravel bar," I cried, as we approached the small gravel island surrounded on all sides by the water. "It's a puppy, Greg. Someone has abandoned that poor little animal right there on the gravel bar!"

"Well, they probably knew you'd be out on the river today, Mom," my son said, as he maneuvered the boat to the gravel bar. I jumped into the shallow water and rushed to the crying, black puppy, scooping it up into my arms. The puppy whimpered as I got back into the boat with it.

"It's a little female, and she's covered with some sort of grease," I said, as it rubbed off all over me. "It smells like motor oil. Now why would someone douse this puppy with motor oil?" The puppy whimpered again, then settled into my lap quietly, while I kept stroking its back the rest of the way home.

As it turned out, the little foundling was infested with fleas, so a thorough bath and a health check were in order. "It's part

Lab, and part who-knows-what," the vet said the following day. "But it's in good health." After her puppy shots, I took the foundling home again, where she would join my animal menagerie.

I named her Blackie, but call her Yuppie, and she turned out to be the most faithful, watchful and loving companion one could ask for. And last year Yuppie repaid my good deed with a good deed of her own.

We were taking a walk in the woods together, as we often do, for I love the woods, when I stepped over a fallen log. The next thing I knew was that Blackie had rushed to my side and grabbed hold of something. It was a copperhead snake that was about to grab hold of me! I shrieked and ran from the area, and soon Blackie was right behind me. When we got back to the yard, I was about to properly thank her for saving me from a venomous snake bite, when I noticed her head was already swelling! She had been bitten right on her head!

Of course, I called the vet, but he reassured me that dogs, unlike humans, get over a venomous snake bite on their own. All I could do was make her as comfortable as possible, while she laid around for a week with her head and body swelled three times their normal size. And I did just that, and soon she was back to her normal, playful self. But I found out later that they do have an anti-venom serum for dogs and cats, and Blackie was lucky to survive without help. Had I known about it five years ago, I would have taken my sweet dog for that shot, and it would have, no doubt, cut down on the misery she was feeling for several days!

I do believe that God meant us to be together, Blackie and me, and I have always believed that good deeds get their just reward in the end. Of course, Blackie has proven that!

Mo-tzu

MYRA A. KOSAK

$\mathcal{B}$efore I came into my husband's life there was Mo-tzu. No, not the ancient Chinese philosopher who believed in a supreme Will of Heaven, which should be fulfilled by practicing love. It was Mo-tzu, his beloved red Chow-Chow, who was named after the eminent thinker.

My husband teases me to this day that had Mo-tzu not accepted me the first time "dog and woman" met, we would never have married. Maybe that sounds crazy to some people, but Mo-tzu was intelligent and had a natural instinct of knowing who was of questionable character.

Chows have the reputation of being aggressive, but as the caretaker of Chow-Chows I've found them to be very loving and protective of their human and animal family members. As well as being the head of our animal household, Mo-tzu was also our resident peacemaker. When my Doberman, Maggie, would fight with Coco, my blind Poodle, Mo-tzu would step in and place his mouth around Maggie's muzzle. Gently but firmly he would squeeze her muzzle while telling her in a soft throaty growl to stop. Never once did he scratch or break her skin with his teeth. Maggie would comply with Mo-tzu's request and leave Coco alone. Often, while defending himself from Maggie, Coco would have no idea that he was actually biting and yanking out fur of his protector, Mo-tzu.

In reality, Mo-tzu wasn't perfect and he did have his little quirks. If Mo-tzu wanted something and he didn't get his way, watch out! One Saturday afternoon, while getting ready to run errands, I placed the pile of clothes I was about to take to the dry cleaners on the sofa next to the front door. Mo-tzu was asking to come along for a car ride and I told him no because I was going to see my father in the hospital that day. I brought some things out to my car; when I came back into the house Mo-tzu had my wool pants in his mouth and was shaking them like a rag doll. Next to him on the floor was my silk dress which he had shredded. It was no coincidence that none of my husband's clothes were touched. I was the target that day of Mo-tzu's displeasure.

We were living in a rural area of northern New Jersey where the houses were spread out and there was a lot of open space. It was our routine to take Mo-tzu for a walk two times a day. Because I didn't feel comfortable going out at night by myself, most nights my husband would walk Mo-tzu. On one particular evening we were planning to go out for dinner and my husband asked if I would walk Mo-tzu while he finished getting ready. I put on my coat, grabbed the leash and Mo-tzu was at the front door, ready to go.

Although it was only 7 p.m., it was an overcast night in February and was very dark. We walked down the dirt driveway, out to the road and crossed so we would be facing any oncoming traffic, and started on our usual path. We would walk up the road anywhere from a quarter to a half mile until Mo-tzu "found" his spot. Once he relieved himself we would turn around and head back home. It was cold and all I was thinking of was that I wished Mo-tzu would find his spot quickly so I could get back in the warm house.

We had only walked a few steps when suddenly Mo-tzu pivoted, bolting into the darkness behind me. He began growling and barking while pulling me along with him. It was then that I heard a young man's voice in the darkness yell, "She's got that dog! Let's get out of here." I could hear two people running away from us. Apparently, whoever they were knew who I was and thought I was walking alone. When Mo-tzu was satisfied I was no longer in danger, we continued our walk. He found his spot and we went home.

I never saw anyone that night, but a month prior to my walk with Mo-tzu our house was broken into by neighborhood teens. I suspect the boys who had broken into our house were the same ones on the road that night. A week later two teenage boys walked in the front door of a house approximately a quarter mile away from ours. Thinking the woman was home alone, they proceeded up the stairs toward her. She began yelling for her husband and the boys turned and ran out of the house. Little did they know, her husband wasn't home. Thanks to the woman's quick thinking, she managed to scare them off by making them believe her husband was there.

Thanks to Mo-tzu, I was kept out of harm's way that evening and for the remaining time we lived in that house. Mo-tzu wasn't only Coco's guardian angel, he was mine, as well.

In loving memory of Mo-tzu, my protector and friend.

Zambelli, the Mighty Protector

CAROL WALLACE

My eyesight was so poor that I was quite accustomed to waking each day unable to see the face on my alarm clock—much less to identify anything as far away as the dresser on the other side of the room. Until I managed to stumble across the room to get my glasses, my waking world was a blur.

That is probably why, when I awoke one morning to see a tall, blurry figure dressed in mustardy gold, I assumed it was my neighbor in the apartment across the hall. We had been teasing him all week about the brightness of his new dress clothes.

I was groggy, confused and a bit angry that he would just walk into my bedroom like that. I rubbed my eyes with one hand and patted Zambelli, the black cat who was sleeping contentedly on my stomach, with the other.

"What do you want?" I muttered.

And that's when I knew that the shape across from my bed was not my neighbor.

The intruder moved closer, telling me what terrible things he had come in search of. "Don't scream," he cautioned me. And, of course, I wouldn't dare to, not knowing what kinds of weapons he might have or whether he might use them if I disobeyed. Instead, like a fool, I whispered.

I have heard of someone's whole life passing in front of her eyes when she is dying, and I understood when I realized how quickly my brain started to work. I knew several things almost instantly. The first was that an alarm clock had gone off earlier, which meant that my roommate was already off to the theater. We had such a tiny apartment that we had to use bunk beds, and since she was in the top bunk I had no way to check. But Kathy was always very responsible, and if she was gone, it meant that everyone else in the building was also away at work or school.

I was alone in the building. And my intruder probably knew that.

The second big thought was that the intruder had undoubtedly come through the kitchen, which means that even though he may have come in unarmed, he could easily have picked up a butcher knife or meat clever on his way through the apartment.

The thing I knew most clearly is that I did not want to be raped and I did not want to be killed—and that there didn't seem to be much I could do about either one if this stranger had a mind for it.

My fingers tightened on Zambelli's fur, as I clung to her the way a child afraid of the dark might clutch a beloved stuffed animal. Other than that, I didn't dare to move. And Zambelli, bless her, refused to.

As the intruder moved closer and ducked his head below the blankets overhanging the top bunk he saw the cat. He stiffened. "Get rid of the cat," he commanded.

Now Zambelli, like most cats, had always had a mind of

her own, and I knew that she wouldn't leave unless she wanted to. It was warm, sitting on my abdomen as she was. And she liked the feel of my hand in her fur. I clung a little more tightly.

"Why?" I croaked, almost speechless with fright.

"Just get rid of it," he repeated. Zam didn't stir.

"Go on!" he said, sounding angrier all the time.

And then it hit me. *He was afraid of the cat.*

A thousand more thoughts crowded into my brain, the most prominent being that if a mere eight pounds of black cat could scare him, then this guy probably wasn't armed. Otherwise he would have gotten rid of Zam by himself. But the cat was parked. Sensing something wrong, she seemed to settle in even more solidly than she already had.

Because of that, I risked doing something I had been afraid to do before, the only possible thing I could do in my own defense. I took a deep breath and let out the loudest, longest scream that I was capable of.

At that, Zambelli flew off of my stomach and straight at the intruder. And the intruder turned and ran.

It was almost an anticlimax to hear my roommate's voice coming from above, asking in bewilderment, "What on earth was that?"

Kathy had been up there all along. Even though she would be late for work, she had heard me whispering in the bunk below her, felt the bed move and assumed, with anger, that I must have brought a boyfriend into the bedroom. Why else would we be whispering? So she lay flat, eyes squeezed shut, refusing to get out of bed, unwilling to encounter some unwelcome male in her skimpy nightgown. No doubt thoughts of murder had run through her head as well as mine. But she sat up at the sound of that scream, just in time to see the back of the intruder as he raced out of the bedroom, Zambelli scurrying after him.

He might have done what he came to do. He may even have planned to rape both of us, since from his vantage point he was well aware that I was not alone in the room. But the presence of Zambelli had given me the courage to let out that scream. With that scream, the intruder had two wide-awake females and an angry, upset black cat. Whether he fled because of the scream, or because of the way the cat flew at him when I let loose, I will never know.

But I do know that none of us became victims that day. And we owed our salvation from a fate that would have done more than mere physical damage to two young and innocent college freshmen to the presence of one small black cat that liked to sleep curled on my stomach.

Thanks, Blue

NANCY B. GIBBS

"Stay in the car, kids," my mother said, as Daddy parked the car and they both got out. "We won't be gone very long." They went into the school auditorium to vote, leaving my big brother, Neal, and me in the car. Since the school parking lot was filled with cars, Daddy parked on the street a short distance away. Neal was eight years old. I was seven. Luckily, our dog, Blue, was there. She always welcomed the opportunity to go places with us.

For a few minutes after my parents left, Neal and I giggled and played in the back seat. After quite a long time, we wondered what was taking my parents so long to return. We obeyed their orders, however, and stayed inside the car with the doors locked, even though we discussed getting out to go find them. Since it was getting dark, I was beginning to feel a bit frightened.

Neal and I started to tussle again. Blue jumped down on the floorboard. She was trying to avoid getting in the middle of a sibling war. Suddenly, we looked up at the windows on both sides of the car. A gang of older teenagers, dressed in black, surrounded our car.

"Open the door!" one of the guys shouted angrily.

"If you don't open the door, we'll throw a brick through the window," another guy bitterly announced.

I was petrified. Even though Neal didn't admit it to me, I knew that he was afraid, too.

"Let's get some bricks!" one of the boys exclaimed, as they ran off into the darkness.

Neal and I began to pray that our parents would hurry on out. We didn't know what to do, but we knew that they had told us to stay inside the car with the doors locked. We sat there quietly. Blue propped her head on the back seat between us. I began to cry. Neal scooted over next to me and put his arm around my neck.

"Don't be afraid, Nancy," he said, trying to console me. "Blue is with us."

Blue's ears perked up when she heard her name. A deep darkness fell all around us. "Maybe they won't come back," Neal whispered. Blue jumped into my lap, and stared outside, as if she were on guard. Suddenly, I heard a bang on the hood of the car. I started to scream.

"It's okay Nancy," Neal shouted. "Blue will protect us."

I looked up at the windows and again the boys had surrounded the car. They were holding bricks and knives. They were laughing and shouting obscenities at us. One of the boys put his face against my window. Blue began to snarl. The boy quit smiling.

Blue hit the window, growling and showing her teeth. The boy jumped back. "Let's get out of here," he shouted. They all ran away from the car, knowing that if they broke the window they would have a vicious dog to deal with. A little while later my parents returned, explaining how the lines were very long and the other voters were moving very slowly. They apologized to us when they realized how horrified we were.

When we returned home, my father called the police to report the incident. The officer explained that a particular gang of boys had caused a great deal of problems in that neighborhood in recent days. "Had it not been for your guard dog, your children might have been in great danger," the officer reported. "You should be very thankful."

When Daddy got off the telephone, he leaned down and hugged Blue tightly. "Thanks, Blue," he whispered. We all realized that Blue had probably saved our lives that night.

Blind But Brave!

LYNN SEELY

In the summer of 1989 I was involved in a rescue of a blind orphan kitten. She was a mere five-week-old waif when the call came in. "Lynn," the familiar voice said, "a tiny calico kitten was just dropped off. The woman who brought her to me said that her husband had intended to drown it that very day. She brought the kitten to me, hoping I could find her a home. She came from a farm and hasn't been handled much. There is something else you should know: the kitten is totally blind and will never see. Can you help?"

Without a moment's hesitation I responded, "Yes, I'll be right over."

One hour later I was kneeling in front of the cage that held the kitten. I had intended to provide a foster home for her until I could find a suitable home for her. As it turned out, she was such a remarkable kitten, I just could not bear to part with her. I named her Aggie, and she became part of the family.

Over the years Aggie has had one adventure after another, and proved time and again what a very special cat she is. But I had no clue that she would one day save us from an intruder. Whether his motive was to rob us or worse, we will never know. But we were clearly in danger the night Aggie saved us.

That night, some years ago, was bitterly cold in Mechanics-

burg, Pennsylvania. The snow was deep and covered everything. At three a.m. the neighborhood was silent. Our old two-
story home was warm and cozy, the windows tightly shut
against the winter air. My husband and I were asleep in our upstairs bedroom, unaware that a dangerous event was unfold-
ing outside in the tiny alley that separated our home from the
one next to us.

A prowler had decided to enter our house through a side
window that faced the small alley. There were no other windows from which he would be seen and it was unlikely anyone
would be out on this frigid night. Even if that happened and
someone were to glance into the dark alley, the prowler
wouldn't be seen.

So far, in his crime spree in the area, no one had ever
awakened during a robbery. It was unknown what he would
do if that should ever happen.

In the quiet hush of the night, the prowler carefully removed the screen and placed it on the ground. It was difficult
to push the window open. It was an old window and many
layers of paint prevented it from opening smoothly, yet he
finally managed to push it up. He shined his flashlight into the
darkened room briefly as he made certain the floor was clear
beneath the window. It was important to enter quietly.

He scanned the room. Only a dining room table and chairs
were visible, as well as some sort of jungle-gym cat-tree that
was positioned beside the window. It still gave him plenty of
room to climb in without making any noise. He never noticed
the large calico cat that was hiding in the tunnel portion of the
jungle-gym.

Aggie, the calico cat, had been listening intently to the faint
sounds of the screen being removed and the window being

opened. She decided that something about this was not quite right. In fact, she had decided she didn't like the sneaky way the window was opened, she didn't like the cold air pouring in, and she especially did not like the smell of this strange menacing person who was standing just outside of HER window!

Every bit of her fur was standing straight out. Her whiskers were pitched forward and her ears were straining to catch any sound. Her large body was tense. She waited.

The robber quietly stacked up two cinder blocks and stood on them. He then gripped both sides of the window frame and silently eased one leg, then his face, through the open window. In that brief instant, as his face came through the window, Aggie attacked! She leaped onto the man's face, scratched, then quickly jumped back onto her tree.

The prowler screamed in pain and terror as he fell backward out of the window. He landed on the ground with a thud. Blood was pouring down his face. One shoe was left on the window sill, but he paid it no mind.

He was up in an instant, running away in absolute terror! He probably had no idea what had just happened. He only wanted to escape. Off he ran, with one of his feet sinking into the snow, clad only in a sock.

My husband and I were awakened by the blood-curdling scream and bolted upright in the bed! *What in the name of heaven was that?*

"Maybe that was in the alley," I suggested hopefully. We both got up and peered down the stairs. We didn't hear a sound. My husband whispered, "Maybe someone is hurt in the alley. Perhaps we should call the police."

I nodded in agreement. We both started down the stairs, intending to peer out the dining room window to see if someone needed help. As we entered the dining room, we saw to our alarm that the window was wide open! Not only that, but a shoe was caught on the ledge of the open window! My heart was pounding as my husband left the room to dial the police.

It was then Aggie walked out of the tunnel. She was fluffed up larger than I had ever seen her. She turned toward me with her tail swishing back and forth as it did when she was really happy about something. How very odd! Why would she be happy at a time like this?

As I approached her, she chortled loudly at me in her sweetest voice. She was really proud of herself for some reason. I looked at her white paws and white chin. She had something on them. Why, it looked like blood! Oh, no! Poor Aggie! Was she hurt? There was a little blood on the cat tree, too. Not a lot, but it surely looked like blood. Worried, I examined Aggie carefully. No, she wasn't injured at all.

Relieved that she was okay, I turned my attention to the window sill. I noticed tiny droplets on it. Suddenly it became very clear to me what had happened! Aggie had attacked the robber as he tried to enter the window! What a cat!

"Oh Aggie, you are such a big, brave kitty," I enthused! "What a good, brave girl you are!" I stroked her as she continued to chortle and "talk" to me.

The phone call complete, my husband walked over to us. "The police will be here soon." Once he examined Aggie and the window sill, he was convinced my conclusion was the only reasonable explanation.

One policeman arrived a few minutes later and surveyed the area. He discovered a few tools left behind by the would-be intruder and he took note of the odd footprints left in the snow leading away from the window (one sock print, one shoe print). The policeman just stood there shaking his head as a big grin spread across his face. He agreed that Aggie must have stopped the robber from entering the house. He gave her a couple of pats on her head as she "talked" to him. He told us this was a story he'd never forget!

He also mentioned that a number of robberies had taken place in the area. He said that this robber seemed to prefer homes that did not have a dog. Then he added, with a grin, that the robber would probably think twice about invading a home with cats now, too.

Thus ends the true tale of how Aggie saved us from a robber! Pretty amazing for a cat! Astounding for a BLIND cat! Her full name is Agatha Christy Cat. (Or "Aggie-Waggie" when she wags her tail.) She is now 11 years old. And just as sassy as ever!

Deer Rescue

SHANNON K. JACOBS

$\mathcal{B}$efore I describe the day that a herd of deer saved Tom Sanders' life, let me tell you a bit about Tom and his wife, Cec. For the past 25 years, they have worked as full-time teachers and wildlife rehabilitators. Their home-based center lies at the foot of the Wet Mountains in southern Colorado.

Among the many animals Tom and Cec rehabilitate are orphaned fawns. When the fawns become old enough to survive on their own, they are released into the nearby mountains, often into the care of previously rehabilitated does. Cec and Tom have a special bond with these animals they have cared for and kept wild.

Early one spring two years ago, Tom decided to ride his horse alone in an area that was close to home but far from anyone else. When he got off the horse to open a gate, then started to climb back on the saddle, the animal spooked and bucked. Tom was hit full-force in the pelvis with the saddle horn—twice. He heard a crunch, felt excruciating pain, and knew something was badly broken.

Carefully sliding off the saddle, Tom lowered himself to the ground. He propped himself up with one hand on the frozen ground and called 911 on his cell phone. While trying to describe his exact location to the operator, he noticed the battery was getting low and hung up quickly.

Tom spent almost an hour in that exhausting position, slowly going into shock. At some point he saw a herd of mule deer grazing nearby. They moved closer to him, staying about 30 feet away. Their presence gave Tom a feeling of peace as well as the strength to endure.

When Tom heard the emergency vehicle down below the ridge, he couldn't move to signal the rescuers, and they couldn't see him. He was terrified that they wouldn't find him in time. He was bleeding internally and could feel life draining from him.

Just then the deer trotted to the edge of the ridge. When they got the attention of the rescuers below, they bounded off past Tom. By following the deer, the rescuers soon found Tom. They carried him on a stretcher to the ambulance, then rushed him to a trauma center in Denver for surgery.

Meanwhile, my new book, *Healers of the Wild,* had just been printed. Tom and Cec were among many U.S. wildlife rehabilitators I had interviewed for it. (A photo of them feeding 12 fawns graces the cover.) I immediately called Cec, and she asked me to cheer Tom up with a copy of the book, so my husband and I hurried to the hospital's Intensive Care Unit.

Thankfully, the nurses let us in. We found Tom asleep, so I left the book on the night stand and started to tiptoe away. He woke up. I showed him the book, then kissed his cheek, and we left. When I looked back, I saw Tom smiling, holding the book to his heart.

There is no question in my mind that those deer saved Tom Sanders' life. If you knew how sweet and generous this man is, you'd understand why my voice catches every time I tell this story, and why gentle healers such as Tom and Cec Sanders give everyone who knows them hope and joy.

Search and Rescue

RANGER OAKES AS TOLD TO HARRY E. OAKES, JR.

I started in Search and Rescue (SAR) when my handler, Harry, came to the dog pound and saved me from certain death. I was four months old at the time. I thought the life of a search dog would be easy. Just sit by the fireplace with a keg of brandy underneath my collar, then go play in the snow.

Was I wrong!

First, I had to learn how to read sign and body language, whistle commands, and keep up with Harry's mood swings. I had to know how to sit, stay, heel, come, get down in motion, and speak on command. Then I needed to master climbing ladders to reach trapped victims, rappel down cliffs, and swim in white water. Oh, yes, and get in and out of small spaces.

The most important skills I had to acquire were to track and air-scent by developing my ability to smell. As humans or animals walk, they shed about one thousand cells per day. I know how to smell where they've been and which way they've traveled. If it's raining hard, the rain washes the scent down, but I can still smell it. When a person stays in one place, the wind and air currents strike into them and I can pick up the scent when it's carried downwind. Heat can dry up the scent. That's why I like to search at night, because the scent stays low to the ground and it's usually cooler, so my sinus passages don't dry out.

I have so many more scent-receptor cells than humans do that I can smell hundreds of times better than them. This makes me highly qualified to help locate missing persons, if I do say so myself. When people smoke around me, though, it can numb my nose and make me useless for tracking for up to eight hours. That's why none of the dog handlers in our unit smoke.

When I'm trying to find one person among many, I need what is called a scent article. This is usually something that belongs to the missing person and hasn't been exposed to cigarette smoke or handled by anyone else. A shoe or dirty sock works real well. Harry places the scent article into a paper sack and introduces it to me. Then I check out all the smells in the area. If the scene hasn't been contaminated too badly, I track and eventually find the missing person. I've followed uncontaminated scents that were up to three months old. Usually, to be successful, I should start tracking within twenty-four hours from the PLS—that's rescue talk for "point last seen."

I'm taught to search two different ways. The first is called a general rule-out search or area search. Harry tells me to find everyone in an area and show him where they are. We use this technique if we're searching at night for plane crash, disaster, or avalanche victims. Harry may not know how many are buried under the rubble, so it's my job to find people and tell him where they are and if they're alive.

The second way of searching is more specific. When a human is buried under debris, water, snow, mud, or dirt, the scent evaporates to the surface and pools there. If the person is alive, I can smell this and it makes me so happy that I bark, wag my tail, and try to dig him out immediately. Harry gets the message and pulls me away. He then helps to dig out survivors. If people are dead, they give off a different scent. When I smell this one, I get really upset. My tail goes between my legs and I paw at the surface very slowly. Harry marks the location and moves on to the next search area.

I'm trained to find as many live victims as possible. After the area is cleared of living people, then we have the grim job of locating and removing the dead. Sometimes I'm overwhelmed with sadness and I know how upset my handler feels. We sit, hug each other, and try to make sense of what we're seeing.

In 1990, a call came in one day from the Seattle/King County Disaster Team to tell us that they needed four dog teams to respond with them to the earthquake in the Philippines. People from all walks of life—doctors, nurses, firemen, paramedics, and structural engineers—went with us on the free Continental Airlines twenty-hour ride to the earthquake site.

After we arrived, we were trucked to a military base where we were loaded onto helicopters to fly into the jungles and mountains. It was very hot and humid. I could see that Harry was a bit concerned as we flew over rice paddies and huts. This terrain brought memories of his days in the army in Vietnam.

We landed on a hillside that was barely still there. Mud and rock slides were everywhere. We saw a place where lots of buses and cars were buried. Harry put me to work at this site. As I searched, I could smell humans under the mud and rock. I had to give Harry the death alert and I could see hope fade from his eyes. We moved on and found out later that at this spot, the army uncovered fifty-five dead bodies. No survivors.

During the next six days, we worked around the clock, searching for victims and treating the sick and injured. It was difficult to search when I could smell death all around me. In fact, Harry had some of the nurses hide for me so I could find live victims to cheer me up because I was getting depressed.

Harry was quiet. He kept me close. I could see the pain and suffering were getting to him. I heard him say that this scene reminded him of his experiences in the service. I could often hear Harry praying at night for the strength and guidance to keep going. God was listening and helped all of our team pull through this nightmare. We found 59 dead people buried in the rubble and helped to treat 289 injured.

The death toll went up to sixteen hundred people with thousands of others left injured and homeless. We did the best we could, working through fourteen aftershocks, rock and mud slides, heat, snakes, insects, and disease.

The day before we left, we visited the Filipino Palace and met with the woman who was president then, Corazon Aquino. She thanked all of us dogs and rescuers for our efforts to help the people. Harry and the rescuers were given coffee cups. We dogs were the first to ever be allowed into the Filipino Palace. We knew that in the Philippines, it's a different culture and they view us dogs, especially ones in the jungle, as potential food. So, we watched our tails at all times.

It took Harry quite a while to readjust to the routine at home. Both of us spent a lot of quality time with each other and Brandon, Harry's son. An experience like this makes a person, or dog, stop and think. You realize how fragile, yet precious, this existence is. It makes us work even harder to save lives.

By the time I left this work, and earth, I'd traveled more than 250,000 miles and put in over 200,000 hours in training, testing, and search missions. I performed my missions in twenty-six states and six countries. I'd found 157 victims on 370 searches and had become one of the top SAR dogs in the world. I also helped Harry go to schools and organizations to tell people how to increase their chance of being found if they were ever in an accident or lost in the wilderness. I was given hundreds of awards for my efforts and was the first SAR dog to win a position in the Oregon Pet Hall of Fame. You might find it interesting to know that I also was the first dog to win the National Association for SAR Swift Water Award because I jumped into the Pacific Ocean and risked my life to help Harry pull two drowning children from the cold waters.

When I went over to the other side, Harry said, "I lost my best friend, my partner. The world lost a true hero."

from ANGEL ANIMALS

This Way, Please

"I guide you in the way of wisdom, and lead you along straight paths."

PROVERBS 4:12, NIV

It's easy to get lost. Finding your way back can be complicated. The answer: let an animal show you the way. Sometimes it's hard for us to put our lives on the right track because we're near-sighted. We're concentrating on the here and now. Animals have a different kind of vision: they look at where we are now and where we want to go, and they travel a straight line between the two. And, somehow, they always lead us to God.

Sometimes Angels Come in Disguise

RENIE SZILAK BURGHARDT

It was a cold but sunny December afternoon as I headed up the old lane leading to the cedar woods. It would be a half-mile walk, and I carried a bow saw and a transistor radio playing Christmas music. Apropos for ten days before Christmas, 1996.

Ever since I moved from the city to these beautiful, wild Ozark hills, it had become a ritual, this walk to the cedar woods to cut down my Christmas tree. A pleasant ritual it was, too— the climb of a steep hill, the vast stretches of hardwood forest, and finally, the green oasis of the cedar woods. I loved it all.

When I reached the cedar woods, I startled a large, noisy flock of robins that had obviously opted to spend the winter among the cedars, instead of migrating to warmer surroundings. And why not? The cedars provided plenty of cedar berries to feed on, and shelter from the cold winds among their dense, green boughs. A perfect refuge for bird or beast, I thought.

I walked on among the cedars, admiring the cylindrical shapes, some twenty feet tall, some just a few inches above ground. Each time I saw one that seemed perfect for my purpose, I would see another one, even more perfect, up ahead. Finally, I chose one about three feet tall, and got down on my knees to cut it with my bow saw. I would decorate it later that evening.

Task done, with the little cedar in one gloved hand, the bow saw in another, I headed for the lane. Just in time, too, I thought to myself, for it was getting chilly. However, it soon dawned on me that the lane seemed nowhere in sight. I glanced at my watch nervously. It was already three o'clock in the afternoon. Had I been in the woods two hours? Then, as another hour passed, and still no sign of the familiar lane, I began to panic.

How could I have gotten myself lost? I had been in these woods many times, since hiking is one of my favorite pastimes, and I was pretty sure I knew my way around. Suddenly, my daughter's call from the city, the night before, came to mind. "A sixty-year-old woman should not be traipsing around in the woods by herself," she had said. And I had laughed at her. Now, the prospect of spending the night in the woods on a freezing December night, didn't seem one bit funny. Tears welled in my eyes as I continued my walking.

After a while, I glanced at my watch again. It was four o'clock. The sun was going down and I was getting more scared by the minute. Finally I sat on a fallen log and decided a prayer could not hurt my predicament. I had always turned to God in the past. He had never let me down.

As I sat there, head bowed, eyes closed, I suddenly felt a pair of eyes watching me. I opened my eyes and saw her.

It was a doe, standing less than twenty feet away, gazing at me, unafraid. She was beautiful!

"I know you never become lost. You know your way around the woods. But I'm not like you. I'm only a human. And I'm definitely lost," I called out to her.

"Follow me."

I didn't exactly hear the words. It was like a thought transfer, instead. And it was coming from the deer! I stood up, grabbed my tree and bow saw, and began to follow her through the woods. I decided that even if this was a hallucination, I had nothing to lose since I was already lost.

Less than ten minutes later, I was back on familiar ground. "Thank you, angel deer," I called out to the doe. She looked back at me, then she bounded off into the woods, her white tail waving goodbye.

Then it was my turn to bound off toward the house. I reached it just as darkness descended. "Thank you, Lord," I whispered toward the heavens as I opened my front door. Inside, my phone was ringing

"Where have you been? I called twice already!" my worried daughter asked.

"I was lost in the woods," I told her. "But an angel in disguise showed me the way back." Then I told her what had happened.

"I'm taking your granddaughters to see Santa, tomorrow. I think we will put in a special request for you, this year," she finally said.

On Christmas morning, there was a small gift marked "From Santa" under my Christmas tree. It turned out to be a compass. I never go to the woods without it, these days.

Ivan

PEG KEHRET

Taj Brumleve is legally deaf. She cannot hear a telephone ringing or someone knocking at her door. She cannot hear the high-pitched sound of a smoke alarm going off. She cannot hear when her daughter, Alexandra, cries or calls to her.

When Alexandra was two, Taj decided to get a hearing-ear dog who would let her know when Alexandra needed her or when the phone or doorbell rang. Since there was a long waiting period to receive such a service dog, Taj decided to try to train a dog herself. She had always loved animals and knew she would like the companionship of a dog even if the home training didn't work out.

Although most hearing-ear dogs are purebreds, Taj decided to get her dog from an animal shelter. She wanted to adopt a dog who would otherwise not have a home.

Taj went to the King County Animal Shelter in Kent, Washington. The shelter had a nine-week-old puppy, part black Labrador and part Siberian husky, who had been brought in because the owner couldn't find a home for him.

The puppy was coal black with expressive golden eyes and a friendly personality. Taj knew he would grow to be a large dog, and that was okay.

She named him Ivan and took him home. Alexandra loved

the puppy, and Ivan quickly became a cherished member of the household. Even Taj's cat, Orca, enjoyed watching Ivan play.

Like any puppy, Ivan required a lot of attention and training. At first, Taj concentrated on house-training him. When that was accomplished, she began teaching him hand signals for "sit" and "come."

As Ivan grew, he seemed to sense that Taj could not hear. When he wanted her attention, he didn't bark; instead, he went to her and nudged her.

A year after they adopted Ivan, Taj and her husband rented a new townhome. Alexandra got her own bedroom, and there was more room for Ivan, who was now fully grown. By then the Brumleves had learned that Alexandra was hearing-impaired like her mother, so Ivan's training and duties became even more important. He now had two deaf people to watch out for.

One afternoon Taj put three-year-old Alexandra in her bed for a nap. Then Taj went downstairs, with Ivan at her side. She stretched out on the couch in the living room and fell asleep. Ivan, as always, lay on the floor next to her.

Taj was sleeping soundly when she felt something heavy on her chest. Still half-asleep, she realized it was Ivan. Ivan weighed sixty pounds, so she definitely did not want him sitting on her.

He licked her face and pawed at her arm.

"Ivan, get down," she said sleepily, pushing the dog to the floor. It took her a few minutes to wake up fully, but when she did, she realized that Ivan would never jump on her unless something was wrong.

She opened her eyes. Ivan was no longer beside her.

The room looked foggy, and she now smelled smoke. Fear jolted through Taj.

Fire!

She leaped off the couch.

Knowing Alexandra would not hear her call, Taj raced for the stairs. The thick smoke made her cough. Her eyes smarted, and her heart pounded with fear for her little girl.

When she reached the bottom of the stairs, she met Ivan—with Alexandra at his side! Ivan had Alexandra's shirt sleeve in his mouth. He was tugging the sleepy child forward toward the front door!

As soon as he knew Taj was awake, Ivan had gone upstairs to awaken Alexandra and lead her to safety.

Knowing that her daughter was safe, Taj quickly searched for the cause of the smoke, thinking she might be able to put the fire out. Nothing was burning in the kitchen. She hurried back to the stairway and looked up. Smoke billowed from around the sides of Alexandra's bedroom door.

Taj now knows that she should have taken Alexandra and Ivan outside immediately and stayed out herself. But that day she was only thinking of trying to put out the fire. She left Alexandra and Ivan downstairs and rushed up to Alexandra's room. She put her hands on the door and then jerked them back. The door was too hot to open.

She peered through the keyhole and saw nothing but blackness. Alexandra's bedroom was so full of smoke that Taj could not even seen the outline of the bed.

"It was like looking into space," Taj says.

She raced back down the stairs. By then the house was so full of smoke she could barely breathe. Taj grabbed Alexandra's hand and scooped up the terrified Orca. With Ivan following, they ran to their neighbor's home.

"Fire!" Taj screamed as she pounded on the neighbor's door.

The neighbor called 911. She kept Alexandra, Ivan, and Orca inside. Taj called her husband, Michael, at work and he rushed home.

Taj couldn't hear the wail of the approaching sirens, but she saw the fire trucks roar up the street. She watched as the firefighters aimed their hoses at her home.

Horrified, she saw the firefighters pull a burning mattress out of the house. Alexandra had been napping on that mattress. Taj knew that sleeping people are sometimes overcome by smoke inhalation; they never wake up to flee from the fire.

Tears streamed down her face as she thought what would have happened to Alexandra if Ivan had not smelled the smoke and jumped on Taj to wake her up. What if he had not gone up the stairs and entered that smoke-filled bedroom? What if he had not taken the little girl's sleeve in his mouth and tugged until she followed him down the stairs?

"Another fifteen minutes," Taj says, "and Alexandra and I almost certainly would have been overcome by smoke. We probably wouldn't have made it."

Thanks to Ivan, the firefighters arrived in time to extinguish the blaze before it spread to the rest of the house. Taj and Alexandra had some breathing problems from inhaling smoke, but they recovered fully by the next day.

When the fire was finally out, Taj and Michael gathered basic necessities and prepared to move temporarily to the Westin Hotel in Seattle, where Michael worked. Taj made sure to take Ivan's blue food dish along.

The fire happened on the day before Thanksgiving; Ivan was fifteen months old.

On Thanksgiving Day, as Taj and Michael looked at what was left of their smoke-blackened home, they gave thanks that Ivan had saved Alexandra and Taj.

The Brumleves lost nearly seven thousand dollars worth of belongings, including Alexandra's bed and most of her toys and books. They had just finished painting and decorating the child's bedroom; now it was destroyed by smoke and water damage. But the losses seemed unimportant compared to the tragedy they might have faced.

Investigators said the fire started in Alexandra's room and speculated that she might have been playing with matches.

Because of her hearing impairment, Alexandra still had a limited vocabulary. She couldn't tell anyone exactly what had happened. Regardless of how the fire began, one fact was clear: Ivan first woke Taj, and then raced upstairs to get Alexandra.

"That dog saved the mother's life and the child's life," says Steve Gengo of the Redmond, Washington, Fire Department. "He acted on instinct; he saved his family."

Each year the Seattle/King County chapter of the American Red Cross has a "Heroes Breakfast" to pay tribute to ordinary people who have performed unusual acts of courage or kindness. A year after the fire, the Red Cross honored Ivan as an Animal Hero.

By then the Brumleves had moved to Kansas, but Taj brought Ivan back to Seattle to receive his award. Ivan sat in the seat next to hers for the plane ride and was given a set of wings by the captain.

from SHELTER DOGS

Laddie —
Hero and Friend

PAUL WHEELER

In 1952 I was living with my Mom in John Day, Oregon. Mom ran a paper route and worked really hard. She got to know a lady with a Collie that had a litter of six-week-old puppies. She said that Mom and I could have the pick of the litter. I was eight years old at the time and I picked out a frisky, black-and-white Collie. I named him Laddie.

Laddie was my faithful companion and we played and went everywhere together. He was always there for me and we were the best of friends. Every day, at the bridge by the creek, Laddie would be waiting faithfully for me to come home from school. He'd wag his tail and lick me all over and we'd walk the rest of the way home together.

In 1953, at a year old, Laddie was outside playing in the yard when he seemed to sense danger. He leaped over the fence and ran toward some parked cars along the curb. A two-year-old child had wandered out into the street. Laddie grabbed the little boy's shirt in his teeth and yanked him back to the safety of the pavement.

The child's shocked and astonished mother was in awe of Laddie's courageous deed. She offered to buy him from me—

at any price! She begged me to sell her the dog, but Mom and I said no. Our dog was too precious to part with. The mother of the rescued child brought Laddie a big marrow bone, as a thank-you gift, the very next day.

In 1957, we had to move to Chandler, Arizona. Laddie was so old by then, all his teeth had fallen out and he was on a soft food diet. He was in such poor shape, we didn't think he'd survive the trip, and we were wondering what to do with him. It broke my heart to think about having to leave him. Each time I looked at his sad, brown eyes, tears welled up in my eyes, spilling over and rolling down my cheeks.

One evening, there was a knock on our door. It was the mother of the child Laddie had rescued four years ago. She'd heard of our plight, and offered to take care of Laddie until he died. We accepted her offer!

We moved successfully, although with bittersweet thoughts of Laddie. We missed him terribly, but we were overjoyed to know that he would have a good home for the rest of his life. To this day there is a special place in my heart reserved for him.

The Butcher's Kitten

BETTYANNE GRAY

I was a preschooler in 1938; and although the worst of the Depression was behind us, our family still struggled to subsist. My mother didn't go to the butcher as frequently as she'd have liked, so it was a real treat for me when I was taken along. I was fascinated by the sights and smells of the butcher's shop.

One day, as mother waited her turn, the butcher's wife came over to me, silently took my hand, and with her finger to her lips, motioned me to be silent. She winked as if she had an incredible treat in store, and I slipped along, trustingly, into a rear room where I beheld a wondrous, fat mamma cat feeding her litter of beautiful kittens.

"Which do you think is the prettiest?" she queried. Without hesitating I pointed to one, although in retrospect I think they may have all been identical. The kitty I selected was then placed in a brown bag and I was instructed to grip each side without crushing the "contents" and to be certain to leave some air space for breathing. Her final words were, "Don't say anything to your mother until you get home. She'll be so surprised!"

Mom stared at me as I emerged with a jiggling bag tightly clasped as ordered. She gave a knowing look to the butcher's wife, and we soon left.

On the way home, my mother asked me what I was carrying, but faithful to my promise I didn't reveal a thing. Soon, however, the bag began to tear and my secret was literally "out." I carried my darling close to my face with care, while softly breathing loving endearments and gently caressing my new best friend.

Each day thereafter, I was given ten cents to return to the butcher for some lung to feed the cat. My brothers protested that *we* didn't eat meat every day, but what else would one feed a cat? Other than her daily ration of milk, we had no idea.

My brothers decided to name her Mouser after rejecting my suggestion of Cinderella and so Mouser became a member of our family, even living up to her name. One Thanksgiving she bumped the outside of our dining room window with a big, wiggling rat held tightly in her mouth—her contribution to our Thanksgiving feast!

Another holiday, while my mother was concentrating on preparing a plump chicken for soup, Mouser stealthfully grabbed a chicken quarter with her sharp teeth and ran out of the kitchen. Not to be outwitted, my mother followed her, fly-ing up two flights of stairs, and cornered her against a closed bedroom door.

My father and I were convulsed with laughter at the sight of my mother screaming, "You rotten thief!" as she and Mouser engaged in a tug-of-war for the chicken breast. (Although los-ing a fresh fat chicken quarter to a wily cat was no laughing matter in those lean days.) That night at dinner, my mother complained, "Imagine having a robber in the family."

Mouser soon became my amusing pet and my nemesis, creating all sorts of mischief for which my brothers blamed me. But I did not love her any the less. We played, and snug-gled, and loved.

When I was almost seven, I developed a ruptured appendix and became gravely ill. I was hospitalized for weeks, lingering between life and death, before recovery was ensured.

When I returned home, a strange phenomenon occurred. Mouser paced back and forth beside my bed for what seemed like endless hours, interrupting her routine only when the doorbell rang. She then ran and approached the caller, bumping her body against our guest's leg repeatedly, while calling out in a mournful wail, demanding, as it were, that she be followed to my room.

This happened again and again. Mouser would knock her body against the legs of callers; first one leg, then the other, emitting her eerie wails, until the caller understood clearly that Mouser was to be followed.

Once the visitor was in my bedroom, Mouser engaged in her pacing routine—keeping herself between my bed and my visitor. My parents talked about this for months, amazed that our cat had sensed the gravity of my illness and was now protecting me, while alerting outsiders that I was at last recovering at home.

Mouser died after the war; years later the butcher shop closed, a little girl grew up, and the cherished family life she knew changed, over time, forever. But the lessons of Mouser always stayed with me. My cat had demonstrated to me the meaning of loyalty and served as an example of a treasured value: love between species. I have learned to care about the ill, the grieving, and the needy; and my heart goes out to comfort those in the healing process. My perception of compassionate humanity was deepened by my faithful, guileless teacher, my cat Mouser. I miss him so!

from CAT CAUGHT MY HEART

Who's in Charge Here, Anyway?

NANCY TOMAZIC

It was mid-March in northern Ohio, and we were about to get our first taste of spring. I could feel a tinge of spring fever in my bones, and decided it would be a good time to introduce my ten-month-old German Shepherd, Bucky (a female with a very unbefitting name), to wilderness backpacking. I threw some gear into the back of the truck, packed in enough food for a three-day trek, and we were off to the Allegheny National Forest.

By noon, Buck and I were standing at the trailhead of the Hickory Creek Wilderness, an area that boasts a 17-mile loop trail through some very pretty forest. Bucky, in her usual fashion, was tugging furiously against her lead, wanting desperately to lunge down the trail. I have never claimed to have the expertise necessary for proper dog training, and Bucky was living proof of that. Her idea of a stroll in the woods consisted of covering three times as many miles as I did, tearing up and down steep ravines, charging through dense brush, and chasing after any critter that might come along.

Today, however, was going to be different. Today, Bucky was going to don a bright red backpack, one designed especially for large dogs. She would carry her own supplies, which consisted of five pounds of dry dog food.

"Okay, Buck," I said, holding the end of her leash firmly under my foot. "This is your new backpack, sweetie." I laid it gently across her back, and fastened the straps around her chest. Bucky stood absolutely still, her soft brown eyes registering utter confusion. I patted her head, telling her it would be okay, and began to strap on my own pack. Bucky watched curiously.

Taking the end of the leash in my hand, I said, "Come on, Bucky," and started down the narrow path. Suddenly, Bucky understood. She had a job to do, and she trotted in front of me. Today, she was a serious, dedicated working dog who was carrying a load and guiding Mom through unknown territory. I undid her leash, knowing that she wouldn't stray. She was very proud of herself, but no more so than I.

We hiked seven miles that day, both of us enjoying the lovely weather and a forest that was just beginning to show the promise of springtime. Late in the afternoon we came upon a splendid campsite, where someone, probably Boy Scouts, had used fallen trees to build a seating area around a stone fire pit. Buck and I gathered firewood, and soon we were enjoying the warmth of a roaring fire.

As soon as Bucky smelled the hot dogs I'd had in my backpack, she started begging. The hike had made both of us ravenous. I took some of Bucky's dog food out of her pack, and gave it to her in a makeshift foil dish. If a dog is capable of looking indignant, Bucky certainly did. She walked over to the hot dogs and started whining. Fortunately, I'd brought extra, anticipating this very situation. "You can have a hot dog, Buck," I said, "but I think you'll be needing more than that, after today's workout." And indeed she did, the hot dog serving as a mere appetizer, followed by another hot dog, three hard-boiled eggs, half a bag of pita bread, a generous portion of cheddar cheese, and one granola bar. The dog food remained untouched. Though I'd planned on a three-day hike, we now had only enough food for one more day. I didn't care. We were having a great time, and Bucky had certainly earned her right to a "gourmet" meal.

We spent the evening enjoying the fire, and by 9 p.m. we both were ready for a good night's sleep. Within a few minutes, I'd set up our tiny tent, unrolled my 48" x 20" sleeping mat, and arranged my sleeping bag on top of it. Then I took my extra set of clothing and made a soft bed for Bucky at the base of the tent.

"Okay, Bucky," I called. "You can come in now." And into the tiny tent lunged my 78-pound dog who examined the arrangements and proceeded to spread out on my sleeping bag.

"No, Buck, that's not how this works," I said, pointing to her bed at the back of the tent. Bucky has a way of ignoring me when she doesn't like what I'm saying. She'll bury her head against her side, and simply go to sleep. And she did just that. I pushed, pulled and cajoled, but Bucky was immovable. I looked at the pile of clothing I'd laid out for her. "No way," I thought. I was not sleeping on that pile of clothing without my cozy, down sleeping bag.

Finally, out of sheer desperation, I grabbed the edge of my sleeping bag, pulled with all my might, and flipped Bucky off the bag and onto the mat. Bucky took one quick, sheepish glance at me, and resumed her hiding stance. "Pleeeease, Bucky," I pleaded. "You have got to move!"

I grabbed her collar and pulled, finally managing to drag her to one side of the tiny mattress. I now had all of ten inches to myself. While holding her in place, I grabbed the sleeping bag, threw it down on my portion of the mattress, and crawled in. "This is as good as it's going to get," I told myself, cuddling up to Bucky's back while trying to fit my rather ample rear end on the tiny space. I was too tired to care. "I love you, Buck." I whispered, and fell into a deep sleep.

Unfortunately, daybreak does not come early in March. By midnight, Bucky had managed to take over the entire mattress, and most of the sleeping bag, I being tightly squeezed into the remainder, rather like a sausage inside its casing. Our relationship was beginning to tread on very thin ice. "I think your backpacking days are numbered, Buck," I growled to a snoring Bucky.

I was up at dawn, building a fire, and making myself a much-needed cup of coffee. "I'm glad she doesn't like coffee," I mumbled to myself, while a well-rested Bucky ran happily about, exploring the forest. Breakfast consisted of two remaining hard-boiled eggs, which I did not share, telling Bucky she could go eat dog food. She didn't.

Realizing that another night like the last would be more than my fifty-two-year-old body could endure, I decided we would head back to the truck around noon, and arrive home in time for a good dinner.

By noon, we were on our way back down the trail, I carrying a much lighter load, and Bucky carrying her five pounds of dog food. As she had the day before, Bucky trotted proudly in front of me, paying strict attention to the trail, while I followed behind, my rather frayed state of mind drifting from one thought to another.

We'd gone about four of the seven miles when Bucky suddenly started pulling on the leg of my jeans, and growling.

"Stop that, Bucky," I said, thinking she wanted to play. She would often grab my leg in the yard when she wanted me to throw her Frisbee, but she'd never been so adamant. I started walking again, only to have her begin pulling even harder. Now she was growling in earnest, and pulling me backwards. I was afraid she would make me fall, and I envisioned being out here, in the middle of nowhere, with a broken leg.

My voice rising in anger, I reprimanded her severely. "Bucky, I've had enough of this!" I scolded. "We're not playing, now cut it out." Bucky barked loudly, and grabbed my leg again. Finally, thoroughly exasperated, I smacked her. Bucky was shocked. She'd never been hit before. Head down and tail between her legs, she slouched off behind me, looking utterly dejected.

I felt terrible for what I had done to my best friend. "Bucky, I'm sorry. I didn't mean to do that, but you're being awful, and I'm just too tired for this," I said, reaching out to her.

"Come on, Buck, let's go," I tried to say cheerfully, but she refused to come to me. I started walking again, hoping she would forget about what had happened. A few minutes later, I looked back to see Bucky still lagging behind. "Buck, I'm really sorry," I called, hoping she'd come running, but she was so upset she wouldn't even look in my direction. I promised myself I'd make it up to her on the way home. I'd stop at McDonald's and buy her a cheeseburger, one of her favorite treats. I picked up my pace, now anxious to get back to the truck, and to make amends with Bucky.

Sometime later, several miles later, I'd say, we came upon a clearing, and in the clearing were the remnants of an old barn. It occurred to me that one doesn't encounter barns on wilderness trails, and we certainly hadn't passed a barn the day before. I looked back at Bucky, who was now lying in the middle of the trail, looking thoroughly disgusted. "Oh, Buck," I said, "I've gotten us lost. Is that what you've been trying to tell me?" I walked back to her, removed my pack, and sat down beside her. My heart ached over what I had done to my wonderful, faithful friend. How could I have been such a fool? I placed my head on her shoulder, and cried. Bucky's tail gave a slight wag, and she licked my hand. How could she forgive me so easily, after what I had done?

We sat there for several minutes, looking like two lost souls, I with tears running down my face, and Bucky licking my hand, doing what she could to make me feel better. "From now on, Buck, you're in charge of our backpacking trips," I said, hugging her tightly. "I promise I'll never let this happen again."

I stood up, replaced my pack, and turned back down the trail. Bucky immediately jumped in front of me, thrilled to be in charge once again.

An hour or so later, Bucky made a left turn, up another trail. There, on the side of a tree, was the off-white stripe, indicating a turn in the trail. It was the very same spot where Bucky had grabbed my leg. Feeling the fool, I followed her up the hill and back to the truck.

On the way home, we stopped at McDonald's and Bucky ate two cheeseburgers, hers and mine. And that night, after a long, hard day, we both collapsed in my bed, Bucky comfortably spread out, with her head on the pillows, and I perfectly happy in my tiny little spot.

Bingo

CHRISTINA CORUTH

Bingo was my brother's mixed-German Shepherd dog. Generally speaking, he was sort of a pain in the neck. He was a barker. He barked at everything—neighbors, cars, cats, the wind or anything else that caught his attention. No one knew what to do about him. None of the remedies we tried stopped him from barking. He had been an abused puppy when my brother rescued him, so having him put down for barking just didn't seem right.

He wasn't a very good watchdog. He was like the little boy who cried "wolf," or perhaps the little wolf that barked "boy." At any rate, we soon learned that his barking was not a cause for concern and no one paid any attention to it.

Neither did I as I sat at the kitchen table reading a book one hot summer day in 1969. Bingo started to bark; I tried hard to block it out—until I heard the back door open. As I looked up, two middle-aged men entered the laundry room, which led into the kitchen.

"OK, stop right there!" I said, in the most commanding voice I could muster.

They laughed and told me not to be alarmed. According to them, they were acquaintances of my father and had come by to pick up the old shed lying disassembled in the backyard. My father hadn't said anything about this to me, and neither man had a receipt.

Being a teenager who enthusiastically embraced the feminist movement, I quickly lost sight of the dangerous potential of my situation. Instead of being fearful because I was alone with these two strangers in the house, I became very annoyed and indignant at their condescending attitude toward me. I told them to come back when my father was home. They insisted that they needed to take the shed, which was rightfully theirs since they had paid for it. Referring to me as a "little girl," and telling me not to get "all hysterical," they continued to attempt to bully me into allowing them to take the shed.

My growing anger revealed itself as I glared at the two, which they found very amusing. There was no way I was going to let them walk away with the shed. However, I wanted them and their silly grins gone. I told them they could have the shed if one of them gave me his license so that I could copy his name and address. The mouthier one of the two handed over his license, laughing at me in the process. I copied the information.

As they were leaving the kitchen, the mouthier one turned to me and said, "You gonna do something about that stupid dog of yours out there? He's in the way."

He was correct about Bingo being in the way. He was tied to his doghouse, which was only a few feet from the shed. I didn't want him to get hurt. I knew he wouldn't harm them. He was all bark and no bite. I held his collar as the men approached the shed. It wasn't an easy task. Bingo continued to bark, growl and lunge at the men. It took all my strength to hold onto him.

Suddenly the men began to jump around and scream, as

they slapped at themselves and the air. When they had picked up the last part of the shed, they had disturbed a nest of wasps. Wasps were everywhere. In a split second, before I could act on my fast-growing sense of panic, I felt Bingo's body press against the side of my leg. He had stopped barking, growling and lunging. He stood quietly, keeping his body firmly pressed against my leg. I followed his lead. I don't know why, I just knew he was showing me what to do. Neither of us moved a muscle.

The wasps were everywhere, buzzing around us. The men continued jumping, slapping at the wasps, and screaming. After a few minutes, the wasps disappeared.

Each of the men had been stung several times. As they were leaving one of them said to me, "How come you and your stupid dog didn't get stung?"

I smiled, "I guess my stupid dog is the smartest one here!"

He looked at me as if I had two heads. He didn't get it. I don't think he even understood that I was being sarcastic when I referred to Bingo as "my stupid dog."

It didn't matter because I knew Bingo had saved the day. His keen instincts saved him from the wasps, and his heart saved me.

No Help in Sight

KRISTIN VON KREISLER

On a freezing winter day, Sean Lingl and his friend Danny Parker rowed a small plastic dinghy across the mouth of the Nimpkish River on British Columbia's Vancouver Island. Rain poured down, and wind roughened the water, tossing the dinghy about as if it were a thimble. But the men, eager to get to an island just off the coast, kept rowing.

Lingl's chocolate Labrador retriever Tia sat shivering in the boat between them. Not immediately obvious from the angle of her sitting position was the harsh reality that she had only three legs. Four years before, as she'd chased Lingl's truck down a gravel road, she'd run into a ditch and cut her right hind paw on a broken bottle. Her veterinarian treated the injury, but infection set in and spread up her leg.

"I'll have to amputate it," the vet told Lingl. "I have no choice."

Lingl thought of putting her down. He did not want her hobbling, crippled, through life, with people wincing and pitying her. But the vet persuaded him to let Tia have the surgery. Afterward, her indomitable spirit convinced Lingl that he had been right to let her live.

As the wind blasted water into the dinghy, Lingl did not worry. The boat's double plastic hull created a pocket of air that would hold the boat up, no matter how much water filled it, he told Parker. They were in no danger unless a hole was somehow punctured in the outer layer. A hole would let water into the pocket and sink the boat.

When they began tilting farther and farther to one side, however, Lingl did start to worry. "Something's not right," he said. "Maybe we should go back."

"Let's do it," Parker agreed.

As they turned the boat around and headed toward shore, the wind flipped the dinghy over and threw them, along with Tia, into the icy water. The men sputtered, shivering violently. To keep their heads above water, they clung to the side of the capsized boat.

"Where's Tia?" Lingl shouted.

He groped for her and found her trapped under the dinghy. Grabbing her by the fur, he pulled her out and set her free. Even with only three legs, at least she'd have the chance to swim ashore and save herself.

Lingl and Parker were not going to be so lucky. The cold itself was cause for alarm: They could not survive in this water for long. Even worse, they both were wearing heavy boots and chest waders, firmly attached by belts and suspenders. If the waders continued filling with water, Lingl and Parker would sink like anchors. And there was no help in sight.

Lingl pulled himself up just enough to see over the boat. He figured that they had to cross about a hundred yards of freezing waves to reach shore . . . and only a few minutes to do it before they sank or died from exposure. They were looking death in the face, and they knew it.

Then Lingl suddenly noticed that the boat was moving toward the beach. Amazed, he looked around to discover the source of this miraculous motion. Tia had gripped the dinghy's mooring rope between her teeth and, with her three legs, was swimming with every ounce of her strength and pulling the boat to safety.

Astounded by her courage, Lingl and Parker helped her move the boat along by kicking even in their chest waders. Though the wind slapped huge waves in the water and tossed Tia as if she were a cork, she gritted her teeth around the rope and paddled as hard as she could to keep from going under. Blinking against the stinging salt, she battled the waves until she'd pulled Lingl and Parker to water shallow enough for them to stand. She let go of the rope as they staggered to shore.

The men's hair turned instantly to ice as they walked toward the car. Icicles also hung from Tia's fur, but she ignored them. She tottered along with Lingl and Parker as if the day were warm and she'd done nothing special.

Lingl leaned down, hugged her, and thanked her for rescuing them. Any dog towing a boat in freezing, turbulent water was hard to imagine, but a three-legged dog? A three-legged dog who actually succeeded in getting the boat to shore?

"No one will ever believe this," Lingl told Parker.

from THE COMPASSION OF ANIMALS

"Man Gone, Daniel!"

RUSSELL K. CONE

In the gray dawn of June 26, 1957, Mrs. Libby kept saying: "All night, he's been out there all night."

I was standing at the door of a little vacation cabin on Dinky Creek, 6,000 feet up in the High Sierras. The Libbys' three-year-old son had been missing since one P.M. the afternoon before. Forest rangers had started searching within one hour. At midnight the sheriff had phoned me at my home 150 miles away and told me to get there fast with my best bloodhound. I chose my old veteran, Daniel Boone.

Now I asked Mrs. Libby for something her son had worn the day before. "Pick it up with silverware so you don't confuse the scent."

I opened the rear of the station wagon and Daniel Boone lumbered down, sneezing and yawning in the cool morning air. I snapped the long tracking leash to his harness. Mrs. Libby came out with a small brown shoe held between two forks.

"He took his shoes off just before he went out. Just think, barefoot all this time. . . . "

I held the shoe to Daniel's nose. "Now, Daniel," I said, "Randy Scott Libby is out there in those hills and I want you to take me to him."

That was for Mrs. Libby. In Daniel's long ear I spoke the command I had trained him to understand.

"Man gone! Man gone, Daniel!"

In an instant Daniel was all business. His tail tensed, his nose quivered, he dashed from side to side of the narrow dirt road.

For six hours we zig-zagged through that wilderness country. Then we came to the foot of an almost perpendicular rock slide. I looked at Daniel incredulously: could a three-year-old have climbed it? But Daniel had already started up, sending a river of sand and rock down on me. We struggled up, panting and slipping until at last we reached a broad plateau.

Faster and faster Daniel tugged and then he dove into a clump of manzanita. A little boy was there.

"Hi, Randy," I said.

Looking at Mrs. Libby's radiant face late that afternoon, I thought: I almost gave up this work with bloodhounds. I almost kept a good job as appliance service-man for Sears-Roebuck; I almost let doubt talk me out of God's will for my life. . . .

A message had come for me while we were searching for Randy. A little girl was missing in Yosemite National Park. Please hurry.

Yosemite was a hundred miles away; Daniel and I set out for it at once. As we sped over the miles, my mind went back a few years. I tried to recall when I had first suspected the job that God had in mind for me. I think God has a certain job for every person on earth. The first trick is to discover what it is. The second is to trust it. Mine, it seemed to me, was especially hard to believe. A dog handler? It seemed so off-beat.

And yet, how else could I explain the things that had happened? In 1949 my wife and I had bought four and a half acres of trees and undergrowth in the Santa Cruz Mountains and hauled our house-trailer there.

"You know, Thanis," I said to her, "We could have a dog up here."

"What kind of dog?" asked Thanis.

"A bloodhound," I said. I'd never wanted one before; I'd never even seen one. But suddenly it had to be a bloodhound.

"I wouldn't know where to look for one," the man in the pet shop told me. "There aren't more than four or five hundred in the whole country." But I kept looking. When at last I heard of a puppy for sale for $100, I bought him sight unseen. A hundred dollars—when we were saving our money in quarters and dimes! It was hard to explain to Thanis but harder to explain to myself.

We named the dog Daniel Boone. I'd had him about a month and was walking him one day when Sheriff Hendrick's car pulled up.

"Is that a bloodhound?" he shouted as I hurried over to him. The sheriff was almost shaking with excitement. "Is he trained?"

I looked at him blankly. "Trained for what?"

"Tracking! Trailing people!"

"Why bloodhounds haven't tracked people since 'Liza crossed the ice!"

"That's true," he said, deadly earnest, "because people don't train them much for it any more. For the past 60 days we've looked for a man. Found him yesterday—what was left of him. A bloodhound might have taken us to him in a couple of days."

That was the beginning. There was no one to teach us how to train a bloodhound, so Thanis and I devised our own system with a can of dog food and one of Thanis' slippers. In time, when I thought we were ready, I phoned Sheriff Hendrick. Four days later he called back. A 77-year-old lady was lost on Madonna Mountain. It took us five hours to find her. One look at her face as Daniel and I emerged from the trees and I knew I was a bloodhound man for life.

In six years we found more than 100 lost persons, from a 92-year-old man to a 22-month-old baby. I bought more dogs. The more I learned about them the more I saw the hand of God on these homely, ungainly creatures: many breeds of dog can follow a trail two or three hours old; three separate times my bloodhounds have picked up a trail five *days* old.

When the search was for a child I would tell his parents my favorite Bible story. In it Jesus describes a shepherd's joy when he finds a sheep that was lost. *Even so,* He says, *it is not the will of your Father which is in heaven, that one of these little ones should perish.* *

I sincerely believed that this was God's work. And yet, it complicated my poor human existence so! My boss at Sears-Roebuck was understanding and let me off whenever there was a search. But of course they couldn't pay me for that time; one month I was gone 11 of 22 working days.

Sheriff's offices sometimes paid my transportation to and from the search scene. But I was buying $90 worth of dog food a month. As for the families of the people we found, I couldn't ask them for help. Deep joy just doesn't express itself in dollars and cents, and shouldn't have to. But meanwhile our first son had come. Another child was on the way. It seemed to me that I had to choose between being "practical" and being Christian.

Matthew 18:14

Then one night I sat bolt upright in bed. If this was God's work, why not trust Him?

The very next morning I walked boldly into the front office of The Calo Pet Food Company in Oakland and asked them to sponsor me. They did. From that moment on I have spent full time working with these dogs, not only searching, but breeding them and teaching others to track with them.

Overnight, people everywhere seemed to know about our dogs. Even the Air Force called: "We'll fly you any place you can't get by car." Nowadays we fly over 1,000 miles to many searches.

And whenever the dogs arrive, new hope lights up sleepless faces. It was that way when Daniel and I arrived at Yosemite that June night. The little girl, Shirley Ann Miller, had been missing for 32 hours and searchers were now pouring back to Bridal Veil Falls campground; searching at night was out of the question in that rugged terrain. Men who had not slept for two nights set out eagerly with us at dawn on June 27. Shirley's silent, pale-lipped father brought along a map showing the areas already searched. All day we pushed back through incredibly treacherous country, keeping in touch by radio with the other search groups.

Late in the afternoon we reached the foot of a tall ridge. The map showed that both sides of it had been searched. Daniel wanted to climb it. It looked like a waste of precious time; the whole face of the ridge was clearly visible from below. How could she be up there?

Arduously, we followed Daniel. Twilight came as we reached the top. There was just enough light to see that what showed on the map as a single ridge was actually two ridges. Between them lay a small pear-shaped valley. But another dark night was upon us. We tried not to look at Mr. Miller as we made camp.

Next morning before sunrise all 200 searchers had gathered on top of that ridge. With Daniel in the lead we started down into the valley. It was almost noon when we came out of a thicket of chaparral. On a log in front of us sat the blondest little girl I'd ever seen.

The men rushed to her, picked her up, hugged her, wrapped her in blankets. For a moment I hung back. I was offering up a prayer—a prayer of repentance that I had ever doubted that God Almighty would fail to provide our few material needs as long as we were seeking His will.

Then Shirley saw Daniel. "Hello, doggie," she said. "Who brought you here?"

The men laughed. "He brought us here, honey," her father said.

I didn't laugh though. I think it was a good question. I kept thinking about it as 200 men, one dog and one little girl started back to camp. I kept thinking I knew the answer.

I Am Here

"Where is man without the beasts?
If all the beasts were gone, man would
die from a great loneliness of spirit."

CHIEF SEATTLE

*O*ne day, as I was having a lot of trouble finishing a story I was writing, I heard my dog Suzy padding down the hall toward my office. She stopped at the doorway and looked at me. I forced a smile, but she wasn't buying it. She came in and curled up under my desk, with her head on my feet. Then she heaved a deep sigh and relaxed as only an animal can do. Funny, but all of a sudden my story seemed to write itself and I was enjoying my work again.

The Power of Pets

MICKI SIEGEL

The little boy couldn't have been more than 5 years old, but he looked like he carried the weight of the world on his small shoulders. Just days earlier, he and his baby sister had been in the day-care center when it was destroyed in the Oklahoma City bombing. Now his sister was missing. And he had stopped speaking and couldn't even cry.

City officials had set up a Compassion Center in the First Christian Church, staffing it with volunteer therapists and child psychologists who counseled survivors and families of the missing. Several psychologists had tried coaxing the boy to talk about his feelings without success.

Then a dog named Shellie arrived on the scene, and began working wonders. Part Corgi, part white Sheltie, Shellie is a licensed volunteer therapy dog—a designation awarded animals who complete a series of special obedience courses and pass a test at one of the 35 U.S. chapters of Therapy Dogs International.

The boy looked at Shellie, inched closer, and tentatively petted her. "I had a dog," he whispered. Those were his first words since the tragedy. Then he scooped Shellie up in his arms and hugged her, before giving in to racking sobs. A counselor watched and felt a sense of relief: "Now he'll be able to grieve," she said.

Brenda Myers, the dog's owner/trainer, can't explain exactly how Shellie managed to help the boy. "Something happens that's more powerful than words," she says. "I only know he got better."

There were over a dozen children at the Compassion Center. Some had lost one or both parents; others, siblings or friends. Now they were dazed and numb.

Hoping to cheer up the children, other pet owners started bringing their animals to the church. Drug and alcohol counselor Sharlotte Campbell arrived with her 9-month-old pet spider monkey, Charlie, and breeders John and Vicky McCuan came with eight of their rabbits.

Campbell knew her pet had a gift for pulling people out of depression—Charlie had once worked with a group of troubled teens she was counseling. Still, she was surprised at the dramatic change in mood when Charlie scampered into the children's corner.

"The kids weren't even talking," she remembers. "Then they saw Charlie. One girl let out a squeal and started jumping up and down. Suddenly the other children came alive, too. Charlie hugged each child—and pretty soon they were all giggling."

After Shellie and Charlie appeared, according to Dusty Bowenkamp, a coordinator for the American Red Cross, "the counselors could begin to help the kids open up about their feelings and their losses."

Adds Karen Sitterle, Ph.D., a volunteer psychologist with the American Red Cross: "The animals gave the children a sense of control. Surrounded by so many adults, the children were the smallest and most helpless people there. Suddenly they had something smaller and more vulnerable than they were, something they could look after and play with."

Myers saw that when the children were too nervous to nap, Shellie would lie down with them. As the dog's eyes got heavier, so did theirs.

But it wasn't just the children who took comfort from the animals. "A woman whose husband had been killed asked if she could hold one of my rabbits," recalls John McCuan. "She walked around, hugging the animal. 'I just needed something.' she told me." Sitterle remembers that Charlie went over to an elderly woman who was crying and stroked her cheek, then put his arms around her.

After a few weeks the center closed, though many survivors have continued attending sessions to help them handle their grief. The work of the animals has gone on too. Owner Campbell is enrolling Charlie in a pet therapy course, and he's made house calls to children he met at the center. For her part, Shellie continues to help patients at nursing homes, hospitals, and an AIDS hospice.

Oklahoma City residents still talk about the special healing the animals provided. "You can't imagine how gratifying it was to hear about the difference Shellie made," says Brenda Myers. "One mother told me, 'My son was in the dark, and Shellie was a passage back into the light.'"

from GOOD HOUSEKEEPING

Just My Dog

GENE HILL

He's just my dog.

He is my other eyes that can see above the clouds; my other ears that hear above the winds. He is the part of me that can reach out into the sea.

He has told me a thousand times over that I am his reason for being: by the way he rests against my leg; by the way he thumps his tail at my smallest smile; by the way he shows his hurt when I leave without taking him. (I think it makes him sick with worry when he is not along to care for me.)

When I am wrong, he is delighted to forgive. When I am angry, he clowns to make me smile. When I am happy, he is joy unbounded.

When I am a fool, he ignores it. When I succeed, he brags.

Without him, I am only another man. With him, I am all-powerful.

He is loyalty itself. He has taught me the meaning of devotion.

With him, I know a secret comfort and a private peace. He has brought me understanding where before I was ignorant.

His head on my knee can heal my human hurts. His presence by my side is protection against my fears of dark and unknown things.

He has promised to wait for me . . . whenever . . . wherever—in case I need him. And I expect I will—as I always have.

He is just my dog.

from TEARS & LAUGHTER

Purr-fect Pals
for Sick Kids

ROBERTA SANDLER

 $\mathcal{B}$ riana Hagquist thought if she brought her pet cats to the pediatric residence where she worked, they might bring a smile to the young patients living there. Briana was stunned and touched by the amazing interaction between her pets and these children, who had severe medical disabilities and who needed 24-hour care.

Gingerly and gracefully, Midnight, a five-year-old, 14-pound, black domestic shorthair, tiptoed over the tubes in Anton's bed. Nine-year-old Anton was an angry child, embittered by the use-lessness of his once-nimble legs and arms. A car had plowed into the boy as he rode his bicycle, and now Anton was a quadriplegic. All that Briana wanted to do when she placed Midnight onto the bed, was to make stoic-faced Anton soften up and smile for a change.

Anton did more than smile as the cat snuggled up to him. The boy laughed, and nuzzled the animal's soft fur.

The next day, Anton grumbled about learning how to use a special computer. A teacher and a teacher's aide were assigned to Anton, but he refused to do his homework. To interest Anton in the computer, Briana talked to him about Midnight, because

Anton liked the cat. "How many toes does Midnight have?" she would ask him. It was a math game. She suggested that Anton write a note to Midnight by blowing into the tube connected to the computer. Enticed by his teacher's promise that Midnight would respond, Anton wrote his first note: "Dear Midnight. I love you. How are you? I am learning to use the computer with a 'sip and puff' device. Come to see me. Love, Anton."

With the behind-the-scenes help of the teacher, Briana made sure there was a response from Midnight. The letter asked Anton to finish his homework assignments, speak clearly, eat the foods that were fed to him, and stop arguing with the other kids. During the months that Anton and Midnight "corresponded," Anton's school work and his behavior improved dramatically.

That gave Briana an idea. She would bring her three cats to work on a rotating basis, and they would serve as therapy cats. After all, they had wonderful temperaments, and were affectionate and gentle. To protect the children from any allergic reactions, Briana brushed her cats' hair vigorously, then applied an anti-allergy liquid.

Hobie Cat, Midnight, and Orrie never seemed to have a crabby day. Hobie, the mellowest of the three cats, seemed to know which kids most needed his soothing touch. His first day at the center, he went right to work. Three-year-old Keneisha, who was born with multiple birth defects, was crying. "It's okay," the nurse said softly. Keneisha continued to cry.

Leaving Briana's arms, Hobie settled into bed with Keneisha. Nestling close to her, Hobie began to purr a patient murmur. A few minutes later, Keneisha was sleeping peacefully.

Briana's cats proved many times that they could cheer up sad and withdrawn kids. The felines were, indeed, amazing cat therapists. Hobie proved it on the day that nine-week-old Andrew rested in his visiting mother's arms at the pediatric center. Born with severe multiple birth defects, Andrew could do no more than stare blankly, his arms hanging limply. He seemed to react to nothing.

Briana brought Hobie up close to Andrew. Suddenly, the baby reached out with his tiny fingers, and began to knead the cat's silver fur. Andrew's mother's eyes glistened with tears. "That's the first time my son has shown an interest in the world around him," she cried. "I didn't think he was capable of responding to anything. It's like a miracle."

Orrie seemed to realize from the beginning that Briana had brought him to a nursing facility. Maybe it was his experience being brought to a nursing home where Briana had formerly worked. There, he was an instant comfort to the older residents.

At the pediatric center, Orrie promptly looked for beds and laps to climb into. The children easily bonded with him, especially 13-year-old Buddy, whose worsening muscular dystrophy had necessitated his permanent move to the facility. On his visits, Orrie would scamper to Buddy's room, and climb into bed with the boy. Later, traveling the halls in a motorized wheelchair, Buddy would take Orrie for a ride, with an occasional time out to rub his nose into Orrie's coat, and hug the lovable cat.

Briana had found Midnight at a construction site near a hospice when he was six months old. Hobie was a stray who showed up at Briana's door one chilly night. Orrie was given to Briana by a friend who could no longer keep him. Briana had a feeling that the personalities and intelligence of all three cats would make them good "working" cats. Their selfless qualities proved that she was right.

The cats knew exactly where to step in the cribs and beds, without disconnecting tubes. They seemed to sense when a child was in pain, or feeling sad. But the cats proved to be therapists for the nurses, too. Many times, staff members would wrap their arms around the cats, and cry into their fur. These were difficult moments in a stressful job, and the cats were a comfort.

Briana wondered why some cats became marvelous therapists while others didn't, but her own cats were accustomed to her frequent hugs and kisses, so she hoped that it was her love for them that, in turn, generated their love for children. What mattered most was that these placid little cats, who were part of Briana's family, had become God's feline miracle workers.

"In their own way," she proudly told her friends, "the cats are spreading happiness and love to children who are trapped in bodies that don't work well."

Our Guard(ian) Dog

ELIZABETH POLK

My daddy, Joe Norton, was a traveling preacher. Back in the forties, when we didn't have a car, he rode buses all over, bringing the word of God to towns that were too small and too poor to have their own preachers. The five of us—Daddy, Mama, my big brothers, John and Bobby, and me—lived in a tiny town ourselves, out by the oil fields of west Texas. Hamlin was the kind of place where folks didn't even have locks on their doors, they trusted each other so much. When Daddy had to be away for a week or two at a stretch, he could rest assured we were safe at home.

I couldn't, though. I had a hard time getting to sleep when he was gone. My brothers didn't help any. They kept right on telling me tales about who might be lurking in the attic and teasing me mercilessly about my reddish-brown hair. Usually the boys had the bunk beds in the kitchen across from the back door. But Mama knew how anxious I got when Daddy wasn't around. She would put the boys in the bedroom, then give me the top bunk and take the bottom one herself, so I'd feel more secure. I'd climb into bed with my favorite doll, Trudy, whose expression changed when you turned her head. I made sure Trudy's sleeping face was showing, but then I would lie awake myself, my mind awhirl with all the scary things that might happen without Daddy around. "He says God always takes care of us, Trudy," I'd whisper to my doll. "Well, I sure do hope it's true."

The summer I was nine I hoped more fervently than ever because something terrible happened, something no one in Hamlin could remember ever happening before, and we needed extra protection. A burglar was on the loose—a stranger going around breaking into houses, stealing things and hurting people who got in his way. What if the burglar came to our house while Daddy was gone? What if he got me?

Daddy didn't want to leave us. Still he had made a commitment to folks out of town and we knew he couldn't go back on his word. So one July day when the sun looked like a fat egg yolk in the sky, we went to the bus station to see him off. Daddy asked us kids to mind Mama, then we held hands and prayed. Just before he got on the bus, Daddy opened his Bible and gave us a short reading from Psalms, his voice more serious than a month of Sundays: "The angel of the Lord encampeth round them that fear him, and delivereth them."

I repeated that verse to myself as we shaded our eyes and watched the bus pull away. When it was just a speck in the distance, we turned and headed home. Mama was quiet, and I could tell by the crinkles in her forehead she was worried.

"Hey, Libby," Bobby said to me, "your hair looks like an exploded can of tomato soup!" With a whoop, he and John took off down the dirt road, their shoes kicking up clouds of dust behind them.

Suddenly I felt as lonely as the single oil pump standing in a field nearby, slowly bobbing its head. We passed our little white clapboard church, its lawn browned to a crisp by the sun, and I tried not to think about how much I already missed Daddy.

Coming up our walk, I heard Bobby holler, "Look at that dog!" I followed his pointing finger to our front porch, where a huge, mottled creature was sprawled at the top of the steps, taking an afternoon snooze. John whistled. "Never seen anything like him!"

None of us had. Hamlin was such a small town, we knew everyone, even the dogs, and this one was definitely a stranger to these parts.

Bobby threw a few pebbles in his direction. The dog lifted his massive head, half-perking one ear, and surveyed us lazily, as if we were on *his* porch.

Holding tight to Mama's hand, I approached the dog and warily started up the steps. "Those black spots on top of his gold fur," I said. "He kind of looks like Mrs. McDonald's hat . . . you know, the one she wears to church."

"He sure is ugly," John agreed.

"Go away, dog!" Mama commanded. "Scat!"

The dog didn't budge. He just stared at us with those black eyes that were as shiny as marbles. Sighing, Mama stepped over him, turned and lifted me across his bulk. John was right behind us. Bobby poked the dog with his foot before he jumped over him.

Creeeak. Mama opened the screen door. "Just leave him be," she said. "Soon as he figures out we can't feed him, he'll go away."

But he didn't. That night, after we said our prayers and went to bed, the dog occupied my mind even more than the burglar did. I wondered if he'd still be there when we woke up. Sure enough, he was. We tried to shoo him away, but he paid us no mind. When Bobby nudged him, the dog didn't so much as blink. That night I checked outside before I went to bed, and he was lying on the front porch in the same spot. He stayed there for several days straight. I never once saw him leave the porch.

Before we knew it, Mama was telling us, "Daddy's due back tomorrow." That evening the crinkles in Mama's forehead smoothed out, and she smiled a lot during dinner. One more night till Daddy came home. One more night till I didn't have to be scared of the burglar breaking into our house.

It got dark out, and Mama gathered us around the kitchen table to pray. We asked God to keep us all safe—Daddy on the road, and the four of us at home. Mama sent us off to bed with a reminder. "Remember the psalm your daddy gave us," she said. "The angel of the Lord is looking out for us."

I climbed up the ladder into my bunk with my Trudy doll and turned her head so she was sleeping. Then I laid my own head on the pillow. Mama switched off the light and went to tell John and Bobby good-night. When she came back, she flipped on the floor fan, pulled back the sheets and slid into the bottom bunk.

"Night, Mama," I said, swinging my hand over the side of the bed.

Mama reached up and squeezed my hand. "Night, Libby. Sleep tight."

The light from the alley behind our house shone into the room and hit the blades of the fan, making strange, shifting silhouettes on the wall. Sometimes I pretended they were people dancing at a fancy ball, but that night they looked more like a gang of burglars coming after me. I yanked the covers up so no one could see me. *Daddy, I wish you were here.*

Creeeak. What was *that?* It sounded like the screen door in back. I peeked over the edge of my covers. A looming shadow moved across the wall as the back door eased opened.

"Mama!" I hissed, my heart thumping so loud I was sure the burglar could hear.

"Shh," she said. "I see him!"

I closed my eyes tight, not wanting to witness what the burglar would do to us. "God, help us, please!" I whispered, hugging Trudy against me.

At that moment, I heard a sharp bark. Then a low, menacing growl. Closer and closer it came. Suddenly it stopped.

I couldn't stand it anymore. I opened my eyes and turned toward the door. Mama leaped out of bed and grabbed a knife from the kitchen drawer. I cringed as she opened the door all the way.

Only there was no burglar out back. Just the dog. The extra-large, funny-looking, black-and-gold dog who had camped out on our front porch and refused to move for anything, except.... Except he'd run all the way around back and leaped the fence to protect us from the intruder. Now the dog was sitting there at our back door, facing us calmly, as if nothing had happened.

Mama gave him a pat on the head and closed the door. She put the knife away and got into bed. "The dog is keeping watch, Libby, so we're safe. Go to sleep."

And that was what I did.

I woke to the sun shining in my eyes. *Daddy's coming home!* I turned Trudy's head so she was smiling and climbed down the ladder. Mama's bed was already made. Hearing a noise from the front porch, I peeked outside. Mama was out there talking to the dog, who had returned to his usual spot. She'd given him a bowl of water and fixed some biscuits and gravy for him. I couldn't make out what she was saying, but I figured it must have been something along the lines of what I was thinking. *You're our angel, dog. Thank you.*

Three o'clock that afternoon we went to the bus station to meet Daddy. As soon as he stepped off the bus, I ran to him.

"Hi, girl!" Daddy said, whirling me around in his arms. "I missed you."

"I missed you too," I said. "You gotta see our new dog. He saved us from the burglar!"

All the way home, John and Bobby and I talked about the dog. How big and distinctive-looking he was. How brave. We couldn't wait for Daddy to see for himself. But when he came up to our house, the dog wasn't on the porch. He wasn't out back. He wasn't anywhere to be seen.

I thought the dog might turn up the next time Daddy went away, but he never visited our house again. I guess he didn't have to, because by that point I'd learned that even though Daddy couldn't be there every second to protect us, the God he preached about always was, standing guard with his angels, who come in all shapes and sizes and colors.

from ANGELS ON EARTH

The Cat Who Played Nursemaid

CAROL WALLACE

$\mathcal{P}$oor Buckle was not a cute kitten. He wasn't homely, just not cute. As a tiny kitten he looked more like a very small mature cat.

His plainness was made more obvious when he played with our other cat, a tiny gray tiger named Eep. We had found her one day, walking down a sidewalk, sniffing clover blossoms and uttering soft little "eeeps" as she walked. It was instant love.

The relationship between Buckle and Eep was also love at first sight. They were inseparable.

Buckle grew. Eep didn't. They came to look like cat and tiny kitten although they were age-mates. Then I noticed that little Eep wasn't playing any more. She grew quiet—and Buckle stayed quiet with her.

It was leukemia. Eep was beyond help when finally diagnosed and had only a few weeks to live. Buckle stayed with her. When Eep grew too weak to clean her own fur, Buckle licked it for her. He was like an expert private-duty nurse, with the special addition of a good dose of pure love.

Love can do only so much. One day Eep seemed a bit

more playful, and I held her on my lap and let her swat at the dangles on my necklace. "She's getting better!" I told Buckle, who stayed at my side. He only looked at me with those cats' eyes full of terrible wisdom.

Eep died that night.

Buckle stayed by her, and when she was still, stroked her just once with a gentle paw. Then he turned away and began to lick my hand.

I had undervalued him, it is clear. What affection he had that first year came from his poor little companion—and now he had no one. But he didn't bear grudges. In fact, he stayed with me as long as I needed comforting, and soon I found myself lifting him onto my lap and stroking him and learning to love him. Yet he needed comforting as much as I did.

For the longest time he would stare mournfully out the window. He was lonely, and I would have loved to get him a new cat, but he too tested positive for feline leukemia. This loving, generous little cat was also a potential killer whose danger quotient increased the more he might love another feline companion.

So he had to make do with me.

We rubbed along comfortably enough, he forgiving my earlier coolness and I learning to appreciate his generous nature. In fact, he awed me when I finally took time to get to know him. How many cats do you know who, when you utter a gentle "no-no," actually stop? Or who run back and forth until you discover the vase they broke and then sit dejectedly, trying to apologize?

Buckle never was cute—he was something much better than cute.

There came a day when I was sitting at my computer, with

Buckle as a furry foot-warmer beside me, when I began to feel truly awful. So awful that I couldn't even manage to call to my husband downstairs for help. I staggered into the bedroom and lay down—and Buckle dashed down the steps and rushed back and forth until my husband finally followed him to see what he was trying to say.

I spent two weeks in that guest room—and Buckle stayed as close by me as he had with Eep. My husband forbade him the bed, black cats not mixing well with white matelassé bedding. But Buckle and I found a compromise. While my husband was at school, he cuddled next to me. When the door opened and my husband came back from class, Buckle leaped off the bed. But he stayed at the side of the bed, as close as he could get.

He became my little best friend. We were good for each other. I enjoyed the little subterfuges with which he fooled my husband. They formed a bond between us. And Buckle seemed to value his role as friend and nursemaid. So much so that he lived eight years beyond the estimated life expectancy of a cat with feline leukemia. The vet re-tested him to see if he might have made a mistake. He hadn't. It's just that Buckle felt needed—and so compelled to stay as long as he could.

In the eighth year he began to fail. His black fur became dull and matted. Chemotherapy produced what seemed like instant rebounds, but they lasted for shorter and shorter times. And then he was gone—stretched out as though he had been trying to climb the steps to be next to me one last time. His will power and determination ran out.

But he demonstrated to me one of the most valuable lessons I ever learned, one that I knew intellectually but found hard to practice in actuality. It's a lesson I wish I had learned earlier, and that we all would do well to heed. Cute is meaningless if there isn't a loving heart and a giving soul behind it. With that heart and soul, even the homeliest of cats or people is beautiful beyond measure. Buckle was the most beautiful of cats, and among the best of my friends.

Omar Khayyam

ROBERTA SANDLER

The little Shetland sheepdog, although only four months old, was bigger and older than the other puppies in the pet shop. I laughed when I first saw him in his cage. His hair was short and in need of a combing. He reminded me of the way my husband Marty looked when he awakened in the morning. Maybe that's why we took this lively little Sheltie home. Marty had a name picked out—Omar Khayyam—in honor of his favorite poem.

Omar was skittish when he first set foot into our house. The new surroundings frightened him, but he immediately padded over to our eight-month-old daughter Lori, whom we had placed on a blanket on the carpet, and he curled himself up against her. It was the beginning of a devoted relationship.

In the beginning, I was unaware that Omar seemed to believe that he was put on earth to become Lori's guardian. Part of my daily routine was to put Lori into her baby carriage for her afternoon nap, and to place the carriage on the backyard patio. During the hour or 90 minutes that she slept, I'd do some housework, or read a book in the family room, but even with the patio door open, I didn't always hear Lori's cries when she awakened. I'd have to check on her every few minutes.

The day after Omar became a new member of our family,

I put Lori down for a nap on the patio, as usual. Omar had come outside with me. "Here, Omar," I called, summoning him back into the house. Omar had sat himself down alongside the carriage. He refused to budge. Our backyard was fenced all around, so I shrugged and decided that if the pup wanted to remain outside, there was no way for him to run away. I left him sitting on the patio.

Thirty minutes later, I curiously peeked out onto the patio. Omar was still sitting in the same spot, alongside the carriage. I went into the kitchen to prepare dinner.

About forty minutes later, I heard Omar barking, so I went out onto the patio. Omar was circling the carriage. Lori's eyes were open. A tear glistened on her tiny cheek. She had awakened and cried, but I hadn't heard her.

The following day, Omar insisted on being left on the patio during Lori's naptime. Again, he sat himself down alongside the carriage. And again, after about an hour, the puppy barked and barked until I came outside. It was then that I realized that Omar was telling me that my baby had awakened from her nap.

A ritual had begun to establish itself. Omar fell into the role of sentinel, refusing to move away from Lori while she napped on the patio. He watched her protectively, and barked to summon me when she woke up, crying, from her nap. Omar's attachment to Marty and me, and especially to Lori, was constant. He was content to lie at our feet, whether we were watching television or eating, or whether Lori was playing with a toy, or attempting to crawl.

There was an empty field across the street from our house. It was there that we trained Omar to relieve himself. Three times each day, we'd let Omar out of the house to scamper across to the open field. "Omar! Come, Omar!" I'd call out to him, and he'd scurry back home.

Our puppy grew into a beautiful dog, with a shiny coat, a delicate face, and a loving nature. He submitted patiently to Lori's too-tight hugs.

One late summer afternoon, I let Omar out of the house so that he could scamper across to the field to do his business. I lost track of time as I folded laundry, then realized I hadn't called Omar home. From my entrance walkway, I looked for my dog, and, as usual, called out, "Omar! Come, Omar!" I didn't see him, and he didn't respond, so I repeated my summons. "Here, boy. C'mon home, Omar," I called out. Yes, there he was, at the edge of the field. His ears perked and he almost gracefully galloped toward the sound of my voice.

Down the street, there was an unexpected rumbling noise. A yellow bus carrying day campers sped on its way to dropping off neighborhood children. Everything moved in fast motion in front of my eyes. The bus appeared closer. Omar navigated himself across the field. With dread in my heart, I sensed what was about to happen. Obedient Omar saw the bus, but hurried toward what had been my beckoning voice.

"No! Stay, Omar!" I screamed. My beautiful Sheltie had already begun to cross the street to come home. The bus driver never slowed down—not until it was too late. Omar lay on his side in the middle of the street. The bus finally stopped, perhaps 50 yards beyond the pitiful, broken body of a loyal little dog who had wanted nothing more than to come home. Out of nowhere, the bus driver was hovering over me, shoving a pen in my hand, and asking me to sign a release form. Never!

"Leave me alone!" I snapped at her. The children on the bus had gathered at the rear window and were sadly gazing toward whimpering Omar. I was too grief-stricken to lift Omar's limp body. My next-door neighbor wrapped him in a blanket and placed him in my arms. My friend babysat Lori. I sat in the passenger seat as my neighbor drove Omar and me to the veterinarian's office. Omar lay on the table, his breathing becoming more labored. He tried desperately to lift his head but it fell back onto the table with a thud.

My tears fell onto my dog's soft coat as I whispered to him, "I love you, Omar. You're a good boy. It's okay. It's okay." Omar drifted into unconsciousness. My voice, my loving words, were the last he heard, and I hope they gave him comfort.

Lori has no memory of Omar Khayyam, but she knows the place he holds in our hearts, for the photographs and the family reminiscences have kept alive the story of a selfless little canine shepherd who devoted his life to tending his flock of one.

To Smell a Rat

LILLIAN M. ROBERTS

Certain cases stand out in my mind as exemplary of human beings' commitment to their pets. Peanuts Candelero the rat was one such case.

It was early in my internship. As usual, I had the night shift— the emergency shift, the one involving trauma and drama and oddball cases. Peanuts definitely fell into the last category.

He'd been named for his favorite food. He was three years old, with a life expectancy of maybe four years. That was in the best of all possible worlds, but that's where Peanuts was living. He'd been released from this same hospital only the day before, after having a large tumor removed from his groin. That operation cost more than some people would have spent on their dogs, but Peanuts's owners never hesitated.

Tonight, only two days post-op, he looked like a goner.

"He won't eat, and he just lies there," said the nine-year-old boy who called this creature a friend. His concern showed in his eyes; he was trying not to cry. His dad stood behind him, hands on the young man's shoulders.

"How long has he been like this?" I asked, cradling the rodent in one hand and gently going over him with the other. He was cold and dry and limp. His gums were pale. His long, hairless tail drooped lifelessly and his whiskers didn't twitch.

I felt a rock-like mass in his abdomen. He barely flinched when I squeezed it. This was not good.

"Just a few hours. This morning he was fine. He was sitting on Timmy's lap eating peanuts. His favorite food."

"Any vomiting? Diarrhea?"

Two heads moved slowly back and forth. "He hasn't pooped at all!" said Timmy.

Bingo! The lights went on inside my head. "Were they salted peanuts?"

They were.

"I think he has an impaction." Rats possess two large pouches called ceca that branch off the sides of the intestine where the small intestine meets the large one. I remembered that from first-year anatomy class, where rodent anatomy had been something of an afterthought. Another species that has such an organ—though only one—is the horse. In horses, the cecum is prone to serious impaction, or filling with dried ingesta which forms a solid lump leading to pain, constipation, and further dehydration, along with all the sequelae to those developments. I was sure that's what I was feeling in Peanuts's belly, albeit on a smaller scale.

I tried to explain this to the Candeleros. "All that dry, salty food so soon after his operation must have been too hard for him to digest," I told them. "It balled up inside him and can't go anywhere. What I have to do is get it to break up and move out of there." Simplistic, maybe, but Peanuts didn't have a lot of time, and I lacked experience in explaining complicated physiological problems to pet owners. I said what mattered, and what I believed to be true: "He's got a chance."

The little guy's temperature was only 94 degrees, however, and his depression profound. "I'll need to admit him back into the hospital," I said cautiously. "He'll have to stay at least overnight in the incubator, and he needs fluids and maybe a stool softener. But I don't know if any of it will help. If he's still not passing stool by tomorrow, he may need surgery." I wondered if colic surgery on a rat was practical. I hoped I wouldn't have to find out.

Dad looked at son. "Well, we have to try," he said.

I prepared a cost estimate and presented it to them with some trepidation. After all, how much could one expect people to spend on a rat?

Mr. Candelero looked at the amount and sighed. "I sure wish he'd stop doing these things," he said fatalistically. He signed at the bottom.

Peanuts was already languishing in the incubator. I warmed some electrolyte solution and added a little glucose, then injected it into his abdomen, as I remembered one should do with "lab animals." I put him back in the incubator and went to see another case. An hour later I came back to find Peanuts alert and investigating his new surroundings.

I placed a small container of water in front of him and he drank. He circled the enclosure and drank again. During the night he consumed his body weight in water. He also chewed his way out of the incubator through plastic shields meant to allow caregivers to place their hands into the enclosure without disturbing the micro-environment. After that I moved him to a regular cage.

Peanuts taught me several things. One: Many medical concepts are transferable between species. Two: Rats have remarkable recuperative powers. And three: Never underestimate the power of the bond between a human and his pet.

I looked at Peanuts and saw a rodent, something that could

be replaced for four or five dollars at the nearest pet store. He was also a medical challenge, and a good story to tell.

But Peanuts's owners had brought me a family member who was ill. They did not think of him in terms of his monetary value, or his life expectancy, or his social stature. He was simply their pet, and they had every right to expect me to treat him the same way I would a cat or dog.

Over the years I have treated a few rats, gerbils, rabbits, hamsters, ferrets, and two chinchillas. The owners' feelings toward their pets spanned the same spectrum I see in any group of pet owners. Not everyone who obtains a "free" kitten in the grocery store parking lot or adopts a puppy from the local shelter feels he or she has acquired a thing of value. Likewise, some owners of "pocket pets" seem to feel that we, as veterinarians, should charge them less because of the small size or short life expectancy of the animal. I can't change any of these attitudes, and I've learned to accept that.

But occasionally I let one of them change me.

from EMERGENCY VET

I'll Take Care of You

"Every creature is a word of God."

MEISTER ECKHART

Whatever kind of help you need—physical, emotional, practical, spiritual—you'll get it from an animal. They'll make bedside visits, give you a reason to smile, fetch something you can't get for yourself, or just let you know how much God loves you. Just being there with you is good medicine.

Coco, My Little Hero

ANNE WATKINS

Having brittle insulin-dependent diabetes makes any illness hard to deal with, and something like a stomach virus can be particularly nasty. I've had this type of diabetes for years, and during cold and flu season I take great pains to avoid anyone who is sick. But you can't avoid the people you live with, and especially not when it's your child who is ill.

My little girl had just suffered through a brief bout of nausea and vomiting, and I nursed her through the bad time. After a couple of days, I still felt okay and began to think that I was going to get lucky and be passed over by the stomach bug. Not so. A few days after my daughter started to feel better, I began to get sick.

At first I tried to ignore it. After all, it was only a little queasiness. Then late one night I awakened from a restless sleep feeling deathly ill.

The bathroom was directly across the hall from my bedroom but it felt like miles as I staggered toward it. Perhaps a cool wet cloth pressed to my face would help calm the rolling I felt in my tummy, I thought. But before I could make it through the bathroom door, a wave of dizziness hit me and I dropped to my knees.

Overwhelmed by nausea, I crawled to the toilet. Just in

time I reached it and it seemed as if everything I had eaten for the past two weeks came barreling out. Finally there was nothing left to come up, but still my stomach roiled and churned. Dizzy again, I lay down on the floor and pressed my face against the cool tile.

Coco, my miniature poodle, paced nervously beside me. My faithful shadow for years, Coco was my fierce guardian, my foot warmer when I slept, and a devoted and loyal companion. Some people laughed at him because he was so tiny. "Sissy dog," they called him, or "wind-up puppy." I knew that he was so much more than that—he had the heart of a lion! But now he was simply a terrified little dog. Whining, he licked my fingers. Then he grabbed the sleeve of my sleep shirt in his teeth and tried to tug me up off the floor.

Using the palms of my hands, I forced myself into a sitting position. I was weaker than I thought; no sooner had I raised my head than spotty darkness blotted out my sight and I collapsed again. To make matters worse, another round of nausea gripped my body. I dragged myself to the toilet but this time nothing but bile came up. Still my aching stomach heaved and knotted, and my vision blurred. I knew I was in real trouble.

If a diabetic comes down with a stomach virus, it can quickly develop into a serious problem. The system is thrown out of whack by vomiting, dehydration can set in quickly, and the blood sugar more often than not shoots up to dangerously high levels. People have gone into comas with less severe symptoms than I was experiencing. I knew I needed help, and soon.

Coco howled softly and tugged again at my sleeve. I touched his glossy black curls; I was sorry that I was scaring him but I was too shaky to comfort the trembling little dog.

A blast of fresh nausea hit me so suddenly there was no time to sit up and lean toward the toilet. I heaved up a small string of yellowish-green stuff, and promptly fainted beside it.

When next I opened my eyes, it was to look into Coco's round dark ones peering anxiously into my face. He jutted his nose into the air and howled again. "Good boy," I whispered with great effort. My fingers reached out to caress his head and he nudged my hand with his cold nose.

Through the pain, I realized that I was rapidly reaching a crisis point. The nausea refused to slack even though nothing was coming up, and my stomach cramped painfully. Every time I tried to raise my head, I blacked out. I began to fear that I would lapse into a coma right there on the bathroom floor.

Summoning all my strength, I cried out for help. My voice was so weak I could barely hear it myself. I tried once more. The effort exhausted me and I laid my cheek against the floor again.

Worried, Coco pushed his head against my face and whimpered. He pawed at my shoulder. "Get David," I whispered to him. My husband was snoring heavily across the hall, but maybe Coco could wake him—that was, if the scared little dog understood what I was asking him to do. "Go get David."

Coco danced around me, then shot out of the room. The exertion of trying to speak had worn me out. Dimly, the bathroom walls swam before my eyes, dipped and swirled, then winked to blackness.

The next thing I knew, I was bundled into the front seat of the car, headed for the hospital. I spent most of that miserable trip with my head hung over a plastic garbage can, gagging and heaving. Next came the sterile green walls of the emergency room, the stiff, white-sheeted gurney, tubes, needles, and beeping machines. But I had gotten there in time, and would recover.

After a few days in the hospital, I finally felt strong enough to try a few spoons full of cream of chicken soup. Propped up in bed, I listened while my husband told me what Coco had done.

"I was sound asleep when that crazy dog came running into the bedroom, barking his head off," the story began. "Then he grabbed my blanket and tried to pull it off of me. When I wouldn't get up, he jumped up in my face and snapped at me! Then he ran to the bedroom door, and kept barking and barking.

"I didn't get out of bed, so he rushed back to me and pulled on the blanket again. Then he ran back to the door, barking. Finally I realized you weren't in bed and that he must have wanted me to go with him. That's when I followed him to the bathroom and found you unconscious on the floor."

Good for Coco! He not only understood what I needed him to do, but he refused to take no for an answer. I couldn't wait to get home and give him the biggest hug in the world and a special treat. The doctors told me that if I hadn't reached the hospital when I did, I would have gone into a coma. Thanks to my smart little dog, that didn't happen. A "sissy dog"? A "wind-up toy"? No way! Coco was my hero.

A Cat With a Nose for Danger

DONNA BOETIG

One morning in August 1995, Carol Steiner, a piano teacher, and her husband, Ray, a math professor, could barely open their eyes. For the past five months, the Bowling Green, Ohio, couple had been sleeping 20 hours a day, so weak and fatigued they could barely care for Ringo, their 26-pound red tabby Manx. They suffered from fierce headaches, nausea, high blood pressure—even memory loss. Their friends were deeply concerned, and their doctors were stymied.

No one guessed the culprit: A deadly methane gas leak was building below the foundation of the Steiners' home, slowly poisoning the couple. Then something incredible happened— and the Steiners believe it saved their lives.

Ringo, who'd just come in from the yard, began flinging himself against the front door. Carol opened it, but Ringo just sat there meowing. "What's your problem, boy?" she asked. "Want me to come out?" Ringo jumped up and tilted his ears forward as if to say "Finally."

Carol followed him to the yard. There, hidden behind some bushes next to the house, was the gas meter. Ringo began digging in the ground beside it. "Suddenly he stopped, opened his mouth, curled his lips and pulled his nose up," she says. "I bent down and was nearly overcome by fumes."

According to gas-company officials, a coupler in the pipes had eroded, and toxic methane gas was being emitted exactly at the spot where Ringo had dug. The pressure was so high that a small spark from the gas dryer in the basement could have ignited the fumes. "Our home—our whole neighborhood—could have been destroyed," Carol says.

Once the crack in the coupler had been repaired, Carol and Ray's mysterious symptoms disappeared. Ringo's heroism earned him the American Humane Association's Stillman Award for bravery, and Bowling Green's mayor was so moved that he proclaimed an Adopt-a-Cat week in Ringo's honor. Carol Steiner's attempts to reward Ringo with chicken and tuna went unappreciated, though. "He prefers a pat and a hug," she says.

from McCALL'S

The Warning

PATRICK FLANAGAN AND GAEL CRYSTAL FLANAGAN

$\mathcal{M}$any might say our little Pleiades is a pampered pet. Gael carries Pleiades in her own special little basket, and feels that she is a very special being who just happens presently to reside in a little dog's body. She has such a charming personality that she spreads joy and laughter everywhere she goes.

Gael explains: Interestingly, I raised Pleiades to be a vegetarian, and although it's unusual for a dog, her very favorite food is snow peas! She is so small that I have to take each pea out of the pod and feed them to her one at a time, and even one little pea is a mouthful for her. Whenever possible, I make sure that her peas are always fresh and organic.

In the local market near where I live in Flagstaff, Arizona, the checkout people all know Pleiades and her love for snow peas. They are used to her barking at the cashier as if to say, "Be sure my snow peas are first!" They are usually very careful to see that the snow peas are checked from the shopping basket first thing. If they should forget, Pleiades will bark so loud she is sure to be heard in the next two checkout counters. Everyone around seems to delight in this unique tiny dog's eagerness and excitement over his treat, and all in earshot of this snow pea ritual get a good laugh.

My special love and attention for my tiny little friend is

always rewarded with the unending love she gives back to me; but I had no idea that she was soon to save my life and that of my husband, Patrick.

We live in a gorgeous area near Sedona, in Flagstaff, Arizona, where there are many mountains and some dangerous curves for drivers. We were on our way home one day, when all of a sudden Pleiades began acting very strange. She stood up in her little basket and started making some weird sounds. Patrick and I were so surprised at her unusual behavior that we slowed down to see what was the matter with her.

We pulled over to the side of the road as far as possible and examined Pleiades, but we were not able to spot anything visibly wrong with her, so we decided to start up again.

As we slowly pulled into the lane we noticed that we were just approaching the blind curve of a narrow mountain road. On the other side of the curve was a hundred-foot drop. We deliberately slowed down around this curve—and were shocked to see a vehicle stretched across the road broadside, filling both lanes. It seems that a tourist had chosen this spot to make a nearly impossible U-turn in the center of the highway, and there he was sitting, as we rounded the bend.

If it had not been for Pleiades, we would not have been able to stop and quite possibly we would have all gone down the hill. We certainly would have broadsided the car sitting there, and one or both cars would have had no place else to go but down.

We are sure Pleiades must have been able to sense that something was not right. She certainly was trying to warn us of the unseen danger that was just ahead. We now know what was wrong with her—she was trying to save our lives!

If it had not been for Pleiades, we might not be here now,

so needless to say we are so thankful for her alert behavior. Patrick and I both hugged and kissed our little friend, and we bought her five pounds of fresh snow peas that night!

from ANIMAL MIRACLES

Betty Boop and the Gang

PHILIP GONZALEZ AND LEONORE FLEISCHER

Looking back over the last few years, I think that it was right after Ginny and I got our first three cats that my life began to take the strange turn that it did. Up until that time, I guess I expected that I would someday go back to my old existence, or at least as much of my old existence as my damaged arm would permit. Day by day I was getting stronger, regaining a little use of my right hand, although it was limited use and I was still on medication. Even today, I have only about 20 percent use of that hand. When I walk through the streets, I carry my right arm underneath my jacket, so that nobody can tell it's not a working arm. It's a lot safer that way, especially when people don't want you to rescue homeless cats. Sometimes they get a little . . . emphatic . . . and it's best if they think you've got two good, strong functioning hands. I imagined I'd be getting a job again, maybe not in construction, but still the kind of job where I'd be earning a decent living. I thought of it as getting back to normal. What I didn't expect was that my life would never again be the same as before my accident; instead, my feet would be traveling down an entirely new path, and a pretty surprising path, too.

If I believed that my little family was now complete with a dog and three cats, I could not have been more wrong. Although I didn't recognize it back then, my life had reached a definite turning point, thanks to Ginny.

It all started—big surprise!—with another cat. One day I took Ginny over to the vet's for her scheduled shots, and there was a cat in his office, a gray-and-white with a rope around her neck. Some kids had found her abandoned in the street, and had brought her in for the doctor to help her.

Immediately, Ginny was drawn to this new cat, like iron filings to a magnet. She began to make her "please, please, gimme, gimme" noises, and I knew that if Ginny wanted this cat something had to be wrong with it. Sure enough, the little cat had no back feet at all, and only half a tail. Another real winner. I held tightly to Ginny's leash. This one she wasn't going to bring home, I resolved.

"How did she lose her back feet?" I asked the vet.

"It's hard to say. Frostbite, maybe, but there's a chance she was born that way. Philip, let me warn you. Don't go near her. She's pretty wild, and she could easily bite your finger off."

"What are you going to do with her?" I had absolutely no intentions toward this wretched creature, but I was curious.

The veterinarian shook his head. "I don't know yet. Maybe I'll have to put her out of her misery. Nobody in his right mind would give this cat a home."

The doctor was right. You had to be stone crazy to take this cat in, and Mother Gonzalez didn't raise any crazy children. But if I had no intentions, Ginny most certainly did. For some reason, she fell instantly in love with this ferocious crippled puss. As soon as my hand relaxed on her leash, Ginny ran up to her with that old familiar whimpering, and before I could pull her away, she was grooming this decrepit wildcat, paying no attention to her hisses of protest. The cat's eyes were flashing danger signals, but Ginny blissfully ignored them. She turned back to me, put her head to one side, and gave me that old familiar "I have to have this cat, you have to give me this cat" whimper again and again.

"Oh, no, Ginny, not this time. No way." Not another cat, especially not this one. Mean temperament and no back feet? Uh-uh. Enough was enough. I shook my head firmly. My word was absolute law. After all, Ginny was only the dog. I was the master, right?

Wrong. This was a handicapped cat, and you know Ginny and handicapped cats. She wanted her, bad, and she was out-and-out determined to get her. Speaking of "out," I was outvoted and probably outsmarted, too, because the next thing I knew, we were taking the rope off the animal's neck and putting the furious cat, who hadn't stopped hissing, spitting, and cursing in cat language, into a carrier.

Against my better judgment, I took her home to my apartment. Or should I say Ginny's apartment—since she was the one who seemed to dictate who would live in it. I named the new cat Betty Boop.

I never expected this wildcat to be a member of our family, but once again, Ginny proved to be right and I was wrong. It took Betty Boop a few weeks to adjust, but eventually her paranoia did dissolve, and it was replaced by an outpouring of the purest love. It was as though for the first time floodgates of affection were opened in the little cat's soul. One night, I woke up to find her lying on my chest with her front paws folded under her body, purring away happily. After that, Betty Boop slept on my bed every night, together with Vogue, who befriended her. And some nights Ginny and Madame slept there, too. She soon began to return Ginny's open affection. The two of them became best friends and are still best friends.

As for her disability—after a few weeks I stopped noticing that Betty Boop was missing her hind feet. Although she couldn't move gracefully like a cat, she managed to hop around like a rabbit, so she always did get to anywhere she wanted to go.

The amount of love in that little cat's heart is something miraculous. In our home, she serves as a peacemaker. If two cats are hissing at each other, or thinking about having a fight, Betty Boop pushes her way between them and convinces them to stop quarreling. Ginny does that, too, but Ginny can't be everywhere at once.

After Betty Boop joined the family, I began to get a real understanding of Ginny's devoted commitment and her unique talent for finding cats, especially disabled cats. As hard as it was to believe at first, my dog seemed to be on a special mission, to rescue homeless animals who would otherwise suffer and die. I became convinced that she had been chosen from above for the task, and she had chosen me to help her complete it. I say it was hard to accept at the beginning, but soon Ginny's miraculous abilities became to me the most natural thing in the world. It also began to give my day-to-day life a real sense of purpose.

More than merely having compassion for creatures in trouble, Ginny actually sought out these animals to make their lives better. And those objects of this angelic dog's compassion were cats: stray cats, starving cats, ill cats, and especially, physically handicapped cats. Ginny's heart goes out in love to those cats who need her, and she rescues them from their miserable lives.

Just as she rescued me from mine.

Ginny's favorite food is what New Yorkers call "appetizing."

Mostly, appetizing refers to pickled or smoked fish, like lox, or whitefish, baked salmon—her number one favorite—herring, or sable. But it also includes bagels, cream cheese, pickles, sour tomatoes, and even delicatessen. Ginny—as well as most New Yorkers—loves all that stuff with a passion, but she doesn't get it often because it's so high in salt and fat. But every now and then I give her a treat because she enjoys it so much that I haven't got the heart to keep it from her. It's little enough to repay her for what she has done for me.

As I told you, Vogue developed cancer. In her last days, Betty Boop never left Vogue's side. She stayed by her constantly, licking and grooming and comforting her. It was as though she knew that Vogue was dying, and she wanted to make the end as comfortable as possible. Vogue wouldn't let any of the other cats even come near her; the only two presences she could tolerate were Ginny and Betty Boop.

I said that Betty Boop was the turning point because after her I became Ginny Gonzalez's full partner and accomplice in saving homeless cats from destruction. I think what happened is that I finally saw clearly what my dog Ginny had been trying to show me all along: that animals with disabilities are just as deserving of homes as animals who are intact, even more so, because their needs are greater. We now had a deaf cat, a half-blind cat, and a cat who hopped around like a rabbit, and they were all wonderful, loving, lovable pets.

That's not to say I didn't have doubts from time to time. I can't claim that I was converted by Ginny on the spot, or never again tried to turn away from cat rescue; I did. The direction my life seemed to be taking was often frightening. After I brought home an entire litter of five newborn kittens, I had a stern talk with myself.

"Just what do you think you are doing?" I demanded of Philip Gonzalez. "You haven't got a dime to your name, you're living on workmen's compensation, and meanwhile you're laying out a fortune on cat food and vet bills. That's gotta be the craziest thing anybody ever did. A dog and a couple of cats, sure. That's normal, nothing wrong with that. But here you are, in a one-bedroom apartment overflowing with felines, trying to rescue every homeless cat on Long Island, and you're never satisfied unless you are feeding dozens of cats a day. What are you, nuts? How long can insanity like this go on? When are you going to wise up? What kind of future is there in stuff like this?"

There was a lot of common sense in my questions to myself. They were hard questions, but there was an answer. The answer had been in my soul all along. And it was this:

Being a casual kind of guy, I was no philosopher. I had never looked into my heart or examined my life. I'd always accepted everything that happened to me one day at a time, as the cards were dealt from the deck. Not once had I ever asked myself, "Why am I here? What is the meaning of my life? Does God have something special in mind for me to do?" Now it seemed to me that He did, and that my little dog Ginny had been given to me as God's own instrument. Ginny was pointing the way for me by her own shining examples of caring and mercy.

Nothing I had ever done in my life had afforded me the same sense of satisfaction, of rightness, that going on rescue missions with Ginny had given me. Nothing had ever made me so happy, or given me such a sense of purpose, or boosted my self-esteem. Before I got Ginny, all I could do was wallow in self-pity, and regret that I had no work to do.

Now I had a job, and it was the best and most meaningful

job I'd ever held in my life. I was Philip Gonzalez, rescuer of cats, Ginny Gonzalez's good left hand. Ginny had been sent into this world with a special gift, and she was sharing that gift with me.

With Ginny to guide me, I began to devote all my waking hours to finding homes for cats. At that time we were feeding about thirty street cats, and one by one I would pick them up and take them to the vet. They'd get their inoculations against killer diseases like rabies, feline leukemia, distemper, and feline AIDS, and they would be neutered. Then, if I couldn't get them adopted, I would return them to their street life. But at least they would now be healthy and wouldn't make more unwanted cats, and I continued to feed them. So their lives were a lot better than before Ginny and I came on the scene.

Our little family was growing by leaps and bounds, and so were my expenses. I was spending every penny I could spare on cat food and vet bills. The veterinarian was kind enough to slash his fees to the bone, but the expense still took a healthy bite out of my tiny income. I was now not only feeding some thirty homeless cats every day, plus my own indoor animals, but I was also paying for their medical attention, shots, neuterings, and, whenever possible, finding them homes.

I still wasn't working, and I was living only on my disability check, but even when money was scarce, somehow I always found enough for cat and dog food. If there was no money at all, I sold something. Bit by bit, I sold off all my gold jewelry, even the antique watch and watch chain that I was so fond of, to buy cat food. I took a loss on the jewelry, because you can never get its real value when you sell it. And I started to think, "Why did I take all those trips and buy all those clothes? I could have all that money now to use for cat food and vet fees."

It didn't occur to me then, but those thoughts were hard evidence of the changes I was going through, thanks to Ginny. Before, I had lived totally for myself, with no responsibilities. Now my little dog (well, not so little anymore, because now she was up to about thirty-two pounds) was showing me that living for others was a better way.

Knowing that Ginny and her puppies had nearly starved to death, that homeless cats were starving and freezing every night in the streets, made me very conscious of how often helpless animals are abused, and that people can and should do something about it.

What I did about it was give a warm and loving home to disabled cats who in the normal course of events would never find a home. And what Ginny did was to find these cats for me to rescue. We were a team.

from THE DOG WHO RESCUES CATS

A Real Lady

NANCY B. GIBBS

$\mathcal{M}$y mother has always been a pet lover. For as long as I can remember, we had dogs, cats, turtles, birds and even snakes. My mother was particularly fond of dogs. It seemed that when a dog moved in, she immediately became its master. Our animals cared for all of us, but it was obvious that they loved my mother best.

After we grew up and left home, my mother took in a stray dog. She tried not to get attached, but she couldn't help herself. A few years later, however, her best dog friend, Boo Dog, died. My mom was very sad, indeed. After Boo Dog passed away, my father didn't want another dog. He couldn't stand to see Mom cry over the loss of another pet. I somewhat agreed with him. They had many trips to take after they retired. I thought their retirement years were going to be the best years of their lives and didn't feel that they needed a dog to hold them back.

Several years later, however, Daddy got very sick and their traveling days were over. Daddy's health was like a roller coaster ride. Some of his days were good, but most of them were very bad. Paranoia and hallucinations, which sometimes accompany Parkinson's and Alzheimer's diseases, were everyday occurrences. As his illness progressed, we were forced to hospitalize him. The doctors released him from the hospital directly into a nursing home. At the age of sixty-four, he was diagnosed as "terminally ill."

After their retirement, my parents had spent all of their days together. Neither ever went anywhere without the other. After Daddy was admitted into the nursing home, my mother lived in a sad and lonely house. Many days she cried bitterly as she watched my Daddy's health deteriorate.

She decided that she needed another dog to serve as her companion while she was at home. She heard about a litter of Collie puppies which were for sale. When her eyes met one of them her heart melted.

I felt that she had too many problems at that particular time and tried to discourage her from getting another dog. Since she was trying to visit and take care of Daddy at the nursing home on a daily basis, I didn't think she needed something that would require as much attention as a puppy.

Against my better judgment, she bought this heart-winning Collie pup, which she named Lady. What a lady this dog turned out to be! She has become my mother's best friend and companion over the past few years.

One night my brother's children stopped by for a brief visit. One of his children was playing in the kitchen and accidentally turned on a stovetop burner. After they left, my mother fell asleep on the couch. A little while later, Lady ran over to her side and began nudging her.

"Go back to sleep, Lady!" Mom shouted. "It's too late to play." Lady refused. She whined and whimpered, while constantly pacing the floor. My mother got up, tied her in the kitchen and went back to the couch. After she fell asleep for the second time, Lady started barking uncontrollably, trying to alert my mother to the danger on the stovetop. My mother awoke. Lady was standing on her back feet with her front paws on the edge of the stovetop, as she continued to bark.

Realizing that something must be wrong, my mother jumped up from the couch and ran into the kitchen. The burner cover had turned black and smoke was rising. Fortunately, the burner was on low.

I thanked God that he sent Lady my mother's way, to save her life. Who knows how much longer it would have been before a blaze broke out in the next room? Since Mom drove approximately 25 miles each way to the nursing home, and spent quite a few hours there each day, she was extremely tired each night. She was so exhausted that she might not have even realized it if there was a fire in the kitchen.

I have to admit that I was wrong to think my mother shouldn't get a dog. Lady has been a wonderful companion and friend to her. Her excitement for life, while including my mother in her games, has brought many smiles to my mother's once sad face. Her downcast attitude has been converted to hope because of Lady's devotion to her.

Since Daddy passed away this past winter, my mother has Lady to keep her company. She continues to miss Daddy greatly, but Lady keeps her busy and her mind off her problems. She has given my mother the hope she needs for tomorrow and peace for today.

The Family of Miracle Workers

SALLY A. VOELSKE

I've been blessed to have a family of three wonderful dogs who have taught me many spiritual lessons and helped me through some of my toughest times. Before my husband and I were married, we adopted a little Maltese puppy we named Puff and a large golden retriever named Rusty. I'd grown up with the idea that nobody wants to listen to me talk about my problems, so I reveal them to only a select few. These dogs became my private listening club. I could release my problems by talking things out with them. Unlike some people, they gave me no judgmental feedback.

I developed a seizure disorder brought on by too much stress. When Rusty was around me at home, he could be in the farthermost corner of the house, but five minutes before I was to have a seizure, he would come to my side to warn me. I know it wasn't a coincidence because he did this every time.

When I woke up from the seizure, Puff would be lying close to comfort me. I believe Puff and Rusty knew I was scared and needed their help.

From day one, Rusty and I had an unbelievable bond between us. He was always there helping me through everyday turmoil. I can understand why golden retrievers work well as dogs for the handicapped. They're bright and intuitive. They seem to know what to do even before a need is expressed.

At the age of thirteen years, Rusty passed on before his sister, Puff. I was with him when he had to be put to sleep. He was always there for me and I couldn't and wouldn't leave him in his final hour. He fell asleep in my arms. This was one of the hardest days in my life. For months, I was horribly upset. Puff was lost without her buddy, so I grieved for her as well. I buried my emotions deep inside of me because I didn't want to be thought of as an emotional female.

And my seizures still happened.

Puff did all she could to comfort me and I tried to console her. During this sad time, I kept hearing Rusty's nails clicking on the linoleum floor. I heard him groan as he used to do when rolling over. My grief was so great. I felt people would think I was strange, so I tried to keep a happy exterior. Puff became my only confidante.

One night, six months from the day Rusty left us, after I'd had a hard time falling asleep, he came to me in a dream. With his eyes bright and tail wagging, Rusty nuzzled my ear as he'd done so many times when he was alive. After that dream, I awoke with a totally different attitude. I knew Rusty was okay and happy to be free of his arthritis and old-age pains.

Puff stayed with us for another five years. Finally, old age took her when she was eighteen. Since Puff was our last dog, my husband and I decided that we'd go petless, but after a year I needed a new, uncritical friend who I could talk to.

One day, my husband surprised me by bringing home a quarter-pound Maltese puppy. We named her Puff II. She was small, sickly, and needed twenty-four-hour care. She went to work with me and slept behind my desk in a plastic bucket. Every two or three hours, she'd wake up and squeak. I'd warm baby food and spoon-feed her. My feelings of self-worth returned because I again had a friend and a creature to mother.

My little dog was the smallest of the litter, and her body didn't produce sugar properly for the first year. She'd go into sugar shock and have seizures, just as I did. The fact that we both had seizures made me feel as if we'd been brought together to help each other through this devastating disorder. During the period when Puff II had seizures, I cared for her around the clock. I greatly appreciated that the company I worked for allowed me to bring my dog to work with me. The bonds of love, compassion, and understanding between us grew incredibly strong.

Puff II is now a healthy dog. Although I am better able to manage my seizures, Puff II cuddles into my side, just as her predecessor, Puff I, did, reassuring me as if she understands. Her vigilance demonstrates the spiritual principle that what goes around, comes around.

Puff II has taught me not to be so serious and to realize that life is only a temporary reservation on this planet. She's helped me to enjoy the simple things. She's there when I need ears to listen that don't scrutinize what I'm saying. She has the heart of a Great Dane and a gusto for living. She's shown me how to leap over problems and leave them behind me.

Some people look at me with concern when I express how my dogs have helped me. But I believe that everything and everyone is on this earth to teach me something. My little guardian angel, Puff II, is currently teaching me much.

from ANGEL ANIMALS

Greta, My Guardian Pony

THIRZA PEEVEY

"What are you going to do with her?" an acquaintance asked as we talked over the top of a board fence on the thoroughbred farm where old Greta and her daughter Rosie are living out their days.

What am I going to do, indeed? I bristled protectively. Then I realized that to someone who had raised thoroughbred champions all her life, my pony is a rather unassuming little thing out there in the pasture. Not quite swaybacked, she is a little droopy around the edges. At twenty-six, Cushing's Syndrome has robbed her of much of her ability to shed, so her gray coat is long and shaggy year-round. Her arthritic ankles click and creak as she moves. However, there is still a bit of a mischievous glint in her eye and she still tries to throw my husband when he takes the occasional ride on her.

I thought back to when I first got her; a scrawny, thirteen-and-a-half-hand three-year-old. An odd cross between her Saddlebred mother and Appaloosa father, she matured into a lovely little roan mare with a blanket of small spots across her back and hindquarter. Her legs, mane and tail were a rich golden color. She had all the sense and grace of her mother and all the strength and stubbornness of her father. In my adolescent exuberance I named her Greta, for the illustrious and beautiful Garbo.

She'd had a rough time for her first three years. At least one owner had treated her pretty badly, using harsh bits and beating her when she did wrong rather than teaching her to do right. She was overly thin and full of worms. Most of the rest of her owners had been good people, but she was just one horse of many to them.

In southern Kentucky in the late 1970's, a horse was still a working partner. Our little corner of the world had gotten left behind in the industrial revolution. Our road had been paved for only ten years when we moved there. Before that, the only roads were dirt roads, creek beds and paths through the woods. A horse was something you rode to town for groceries or mail. Sometimes that ride was long, so the horse had better be gaited or you wouldn't be able to walk when you got off. Descendents of a Saddlebred or a Tennessee Walking Horse who could rack or do a running walk were preferred. Trotting horses just bounced you to death. A mule was meant for heavy work and ponies were meant for cultivating tobacco plants. If they couldn't do any of those things, they made good dog food. They were often traded in as we would now trade in a used car we didn't need, and there were many dealers in our neighborhood. Horses were too valuable and necessary to neglect but too expensive to leave any money over for spoiling them. They certainly weren't meant for pets. But as a working partner, they were entitled at least to good food, good shoes, shelter in winter and an occasional affectionate pat.

I was having a rough time myself. I had grown up an only

child in Lancaster, Pennsylvania. I was used to row houses, stage plays, movie theaters, the symphony, a library within walking distance, schools in walking distance, art lessons and piano lessons, steak sandwiches and Mexican cooking and Pennsylvania German cooking and ten different kinds of bread in the supermarket. Lancaster may not be New York, but it has its fair share of culture for a small town.

That changed when my mother remarried and moved us to this tiny backwater 700 miles from the only friends and family I'd ever known. Our new farm was 96 beautiful acres of tobacco and beef cattle, with two new barns, but the house was a shack. The old log cabin section had settled to the ground and heavy rains brought water up through the floor boards and carpet. Daylight showed through the cracks in the clapboards of the other rooms. The only bathroom was a tin tub in the kitchen, and the little house out back. Laundry was accomplished in a wringer washer in the back yard. The only kids my age were a mile in either direction. The only entertainment in town was an old movie theatre with a leaky roof that got movies two months after my friends had written to tell me about them. The only bread in town was either store-bought white squish bread or cornmeal for homemade corn bread. If I wanted rye, I was out of luck. I didn't get along with my stepfather and I didn't have any friends. The city kid was not adjusting well to life on the farm.

Winter made it worse when the winter of 77-78 sent indoor temps plummeting below forty degrees with all three wood stoves blazing and cherry red. School was shut down for six weeks because the back roads were impassable and the county had neither plows nor snow tires for buses. My days consisted of packing water, splitting wood and caring for animals in 18 inches of snow. The term "cabin fever" took on a whole new meaning. Many days I cried on Greta's shoulders and pleaded to God to make me grow up fast so I could move back home and get away from that horrible place.

Greta and I bonded in a special way that few friends do. I read every book and magazine I could and pestered every horseman I met until I was able to make Greta glow with health and contentment. Not that our friendship didn't make many of them chuckle, but they gave me enough training to care for her. Her wormy pot-belly disappeared after repeated treatments. Her coat began to gleam under daily groomings by Pony Club Manual directions. Her feet began to improve as regular shoeing got her chronic white-line disease under control. She muscled up and got to a healthy weight, checked weekly with a weight tape.

She, in return, gave me friendship and unconditional acceptance. She never wanted petting; her upbringing hadn't allowed for affection. She preferred to stand close, without touching, and just enjoy my company. The only time she allowed me to pet and hug her was if I was upset. She always sensed my turmoil and she'd wrap her head and neck around me and pull me close as a mare would her foal. Many a time I cried out my problems on her willing shoulder.

As time passed, I broke her to drive and do field work. That also caused a bit of chuckling around the neighborhood. Over twenty years later the story is still told during every holiday gathering of how my two horses got away from me and galloped through the middle of a neighboring couples' twentieth-anniversary lawn party, scattering children, dogs and assorted party-goers in every direction. Fortunately they didn't hit the buffet table. I arrived several minutes later to retrieve the mares from two horsemen in the party who had caught them. I picked up my harness along the road in pieces and took it home to rivet it back together and try again. Fortunately, no harm was done except to my ego, which still gets dented every time the story is told. Nothing like a pony to teach you humility.

We had many mishaps, all without injury, but eventually there was nothing she loved more than to pit her full strength and intellect against a load that she had no business being able to pull with her puny 720 pounds. She taught me the meaning of giving all you had to give, of holding nothing back, of being a full-fledged partner in anything we did. There was a particular beauty in the way she did things that put our other horses to shame. She used to out-pull our half-Belgian mare routinely, simply because she tried harder. I never had to do anything more than ask her to pull and she would move the load or die trying. Many times, I ruefully patched the harness back together after realizing that the load had been too big. She disced and harrowed and cultivated the garden, hauled manure, firewood, logs and brush. She pulled me in a cart to visit neighbors and friends and gave me freedom to move about. The work we did together began to make me feel vested in the farm, and I began to love it, too.

I sometimes think that is why God gives us animals. I think He understands that they can teach us, in a very tangible way, about our relationship to Him. When they are frightened, we feel as He must when we are frightened. When they trust, we see how it feels when we trust. When they throw all of their strength and stamina into doing our will, it is easy to see how God must feel when we throw all of our strength into doing His will. When they come to us for healing and relief from pain and cold and hunger, then we see how it must be when we go to Him and lay our concerns in His hands. Greta taught me more about what it means to love God, to be a partner, a teacher, a friend and, hopefully, one day, a mother, than I can even begin to realize. Nothing compares, however, to what she did in our third year together. In that year, I realized that sometimes angels come in pony form.

That year, when she was six, I bred her to a colt that stood stud in our neighborhood. Then I turned her out to pasture with Honey, a nine-year-old Tennessee Walking Horse mare that we had just gotten. I had bought Honey out of a dealer's lot in which he was collecting horses to sell for slaughter. She was a well-bred registered mare, but she had been foundered and was in a fair bit of pain. No one knows exactly what happens with founder, but it usually follows overeating, overwork or bad foaling. The laminae that fasten the hoof to the coffin bone inside the hoof die and the bone rotates. At the least, the foot often becomes deformed; at the worst it can get so bad that the pointed tip of the bone comes through the bottom of the foot. The disease is incurable, although sometimes, with good care, you can manage it for some years. Honey was bad enough to have a soft spot on the sole of her foot, but it hadn't been long enough to see how badly her feet would deform. At $.69 a pound, it was more profitable to sell this 1,000 pound mare for slaughter than to try to nurse her back to health.

I paid the price per pound, brought Honey home and began an aggressive program to try to save her. My blacksmith put special shoes on her with heels that extended well behind her foot to support the bone and keep it from turning. The shoes would be changed every three weeks. Then we put her out on an overgrazed field, with Greta for company, in a desperate attempt to get weight off her quickly. Walking slowly around the big field in order to find enough to eat would help keep blood circulating in her feet.

To keep Greta from getting thin, I would walk out in the pasture each night, jump on her and ride her to the barn. There I would feed her well and turn her back out. That was my mistake. One night, I found the two of them standing head to tail, switching flies off one another's faces. They had quickly become buddies, although Honey was definitely the top of the pecking order. Being young and dumb, I thought that it was safe to jump on Greta as long as I had her between Honey and me. Besides, Honey had never been anything but gentle and I didn't expect anything different.

Just as I bellied up onto Greta's back, she reached over and nipped at Honey's neck. It was just a playful nip, but in her painful condition Honey attacked. She swung around in front of Greta in one leap and began kicking. Except she wasn't hitting Greta, she was hitting me. The air seemed full of slashing, whistling, steel-shod hooves. The extended heels were biting into my legs and feet, bruising, crunching and, in places, tearing chunks out of me. I gave in and slid to the ground, curling into a fetal ball and covering my head. "God save me," I thought, "I'm going to die!"

Suddenly the feet stopped hitting. I glanced up and saw Greta's belly above me. She was shielding me, taking the blows with her own body. Then she reared and struck the other mare on the back. Honey swung away and ran for the far corner of the field, with Greta in hot pursuit. She never paused in her attack on the larger mare, despite the fact that Honey outweighed her by 300 pounds and was six inches taller.

I struggled to my feet and began hopping toward the house out of sight over the hill. My left leg gaped open and there was tissue hanging out of a wound. I knew this was going to take some time, as I couldn't move very fast. My mother was out of earshot in the house, so I was just going to have to make it on my own. Out of the corner of my eye, I saw both horses pelting back toward me. Greta was holding her own, outrunning the bigger mare. She cut Honey off and again put her body between us. Slowly, she shadowed me, keeping Honey away.

Eventually, we made it to the fence. I crawled under and made my way to the house where my mother and stepfather took me to the hospital. I endured numerous X rays and stitches. It took over an hour just to flush the dirt and debris out of the wounds. The heels of Honey's shoes had grazed the bone and torn out fat and muscle tissue, but miraculously, no bones were broken. My leg didn't want to work quite right at first because of the swelling, but it would be fine in time.

For three days, my stepfather took over feeding the horses. Then one afternoon he came back from feeding and stood over me with concern on his face. "I know it's still hard to walk," he said, "but you'd better hobble out there and see to your horse. She doesn't seem to have been hurt. There are no marks on her, but she won't leave the corner where you went under the fence and she keeps whinnying toward the house. She won't eat, and I haven't seen her go to the spring for a drink since you got hurt."

I hobbled out to see her. When I made it to the corner to reassure her that I was okay, she nuzzled me for a moment, then galloped down to the spring for a drink. She began to eat normally from then on.

Animal behaviorists will tell us that animals don't feel love. I don't believe it for a minute. Horses don't normally risk themselves for others or disobey their social order or refuse food and water. Mares will protect their babies, but I was not a foal. Even so, horses usually shield their babies with their bodies but they don't often attack larger horses, higher on the pecking order. What would cause an animal to do something so against its instinct but love? I figured God must have had some purpose when He gave me a fierce and loving protector like Greta. I promised her that I would never forget her selfless act.

In due time, Greta produced a fine daughter who was like her in almost every way. I made a carriage pair of them and took them with me to Maryland when I got a job doing horse and carriage weddings, parades and birthday parties. Greta and Rosie earned their keep and mine pulling a carriage in and around Baltimore for almost two years. As a treat, my boss let me take them along and show them when he showed his horses at pleasure-driving shows. They were almost always in the ribbons.

When I lost that job and, with it, the ponies' home, I was nearly mad with worry. I tried every way I could to find a way to keep them, but board isn't cheap around Baltimore and I couldn't afford to send them home to Kentucky. Eventually it came down to selling them or watching them starve. Thankfully, the experience they'd gained made it easy for me to find them a good home with a woman in South Carolina. The hardest thing I ever did was put them on that trailer bound for Aiken. Greta somehow seemed to know that she was leaving for good, and even though she was used to being on a trailer nearly all day every weekend, she uncharacteristically screamed until I couldn't bear to hear her anymore. "I'll get you back someday, girl," I whispered, fighting back tears, "I promise."

Years passed. I checked on them periodically, and once even drove all the way down to Aiken to see them. Their new owner loved them and they were always well cared for. I consoled myself with the fact that they seemed happy. I returned to Kentucky, got a teaching degree, married and settled down. But at night, I dreamed over and over that I was riding Greta. Morning after morning, I would wake thrilling to the feel of her muscles rippling under my legs, her mane in my face and the hot sweaty smell of her neck, only to be crushed to remember that she was no longer mine as the fog of sleep cleared. I never forgot my promise to her, although as Greta reached her twenties, I became afraid to contact her owner for fear I would find out that the mare had died of old age. I lost contact with her altogether.

God works in mysterious ways His wonders to achieve. Thirteen years after sending Greta and Rosie to Aiken, my husband and I were visiting a friend. The friend offered us a free trial subscription to a driving horse magazine he distributed. When the first issue came a few weeks later, it contained an obituary for Greta's owner. Through the Internet, I was able to locate the owner's sons. When I called them to see if the old ponies still had a home, they offered to give my beloved Greta back to me. A few short weeks later, we headed to South Carolina with a borrowed truck and trailer to bring my angel pony and her daughter home to live on a friend's farm.

Back in Kentucky, they quickly settled into the routine of a thoroughbred farm. Here they will live out their days, cared for and loved, as I promised. Greta is spoiled now in ways she never dreamed of when she was young: hot cooked mashes every night, full of oatmeal and flax seed, double blankets when it is cold. All the skills my husband and I have learned in a lifetime of being professional horsemen are being brought to bear to be sure that her every need is met. She grazes with her daughter, and tries to throw my husband when he rides her occasionally.

I turned to my acquaintance and replied, "I will care for her to the end of her days, as she has cared for me. Nobody minds if she is a little saggy and rough-coated. She earned her wings long ago, and they are lovely."

• • •

Postscript: Honey's attack was probably due to the pain she was suffering at the time. We kept her for nearly ten years and she never showed any hint of kicking again. I was able to stabilize her feet and get her healthy. Eventually I was able to ride her and show her in the county fair. Her great love was herding cattle. She raised three fine foals for us, one of whom became a successful show horse.

Nurse Smudge

DIANE M. CIARLONI

$\mathcal{I}$t began just like any other weekday. Of course, I didn't realize it then but the operative word in that statement was "began," since the day ended beyond the pale of ordinary.

I was out of bed, in my robe, and opening the door to retrieve the morning newspaper. My routine was to glance through the pages over a cup of coffee before getting dressed and walking down the stairs to my at-home office. A slight rustling noise caught my attention as I stood at the open door. I looked down and there, looking up, was a small, red-and-white dog. Her gaze was expectant but steady. There was no fear in her eyes or in her posture.

"Hello," I said. "I don't think you belong here."

Without so much as a by-your-leave, the little dog marched (yes, she really did march with an obvious air of determination) through the door and into the entry hall. Without the slightest hesitation, she made a crisp, military-precision turn into the dining room and then quickly exited into the breakfast room/kitchen. The last thing passing through the doorway was her feathery, plumed tail that curved not down, not straight up, not over her back but, well, sort of up and out. She never broke stride until she reached the water bowl.

With her thirst satisfied, she turned and began eating the

kibble in Spumone's bowl. Spumone, a 15-year-old West High-
land Terrier, watched with her snapping black eyes. She looked
from the red-and-white dog to me, and back again to the inter-
loper. She exhibited a reasonable facsimile of a tennis fan at an
indoor match.

"I don't know who she is," I said to Spumone, with a shrug
of my shoulders. As soon as the words were out of my mouth,
the little red-and-white number walked to the love seat in the
breakfast room, leaped to the middle cushion, curled up and
went to sleep.

I truly did not decide to keep this dog. No. Definitely not.
Instead, she decided to keep me. That was it. A simple fact. She
was less than a year old. Short. A compact yet delicately refined
body. Her hair was a silky red and white, with the red running
over the top of her forehead and then splitting into two distinct
"wings" that wrapped around each eye. Her muzzle, which
was mostly white, was specked with red freckles.

We didn't know it until later, but she was a Cavalier
Spaniel. I'd always referred to the breed as Staffordshire because of all the Staffordshire dog figurines in antique shops.
They were made in Staffordshire, England, and the Cavalier
Spaniel began as a "royal" dog. Her ears were short and fringed
at the ends. They matched the long, white "feathers" encircling
each of her four feet. Her eyes were a dark, dark amber. Gentle.
Deep. The kind of eyes that paperback romance novelists
might refer to as "limpid pools" of something or other.

There was a quality that was pleasingly odd about her.
There was an air of joy. Her plumed tail was seldom still. It
moved constantly, even in her sleep. She seemed to smile. She
was, well, to put it simply, she was a happy little dog whose
heart seemed to pump with vibrancy rather than with mere

life. When she sat and looked up, what appeared to be a thin, black, smudge-like mustache was visible in the space separating the bottom of her nose from the top of her upper lip. "Smudge" sounded like an appropriate name.

Smudge stayed, and we soon learned she was no respecter of persons. She devoted herself and her ministering to whomever needed it the most. I know many people thought I'd left my marbles rolling around in some dark place, but I was convinced Smudge had been sent to us. I knew, beyond any doubt, she had followed a special path until she arrived at our door. We didn't know it then, but we were going to need her.

One evening shortly after Smudge appeared, my husband was seized with sharp chest pains while walking around the block. The ultimate result was triple by-pass surgery. As so often happens, it wasn't the massive scar on his chest that caused the most serious problem but, rather, the leg that had yielded the vein required for constructing the actual by-pass. It was screamingly sore and infected, and he lived in fear of anyone touching it.

We arrived home from the hospital and headed straight for the bedroom. Propped against pillows, John placed his right leg on top of the sheet and blanket rather than underneath. "I just don't want anything touching it," he said. It was only a matter of seconds before Smudge leaped onto the bed and stretched herself full length next to the affected leg. Not touching it, mind you. There was an easy six inches between it and her red-and-white body, but she was close enough to protect the limb from such rambunctious invaders as cats. She faced outward so she could detect the slightest movement, turning her head sideways every now and then and stretching it over her back to look at John.

She stayed next to that leg. And she stayed. The only time she left her post was late at night when she went into the kitchen for food and water. That's when we began calling her Nurse Smudge.

The days passed and, before too long, it was time for John to begin exercising. The open design of our house lent itself beautifully to circular walking. I was downstairs, sitting at my desk, when I heard John's first tentative steps. Before too long I became aware of a strange rhythm to the walking. Unable to resist solving the mystery of the uneven cadence, I crept up the stairs to see for myself. There, with her plumed tail flying like a banner, was Smudge taking every step with my husband.

Smudge loved her family but she didn't spend a lot of time fawning over anyone. She was, in a way, independent but, really, that's not the correct word. She was happiest when we were around, but she wasn't unhappy if we weren't. Yes. That was it. Besides, she stayed extremely busy with all her ministerings.

Dogs and cats were added to the household after Smudge's arrival. As a matter of fact, it was an accepted fact that the animal population in our family never held status quo. The creatures were constantly being dumped in the woods, eventually staggering into our yard. And, for the most part, they stayed. Smudge did her fair share of raising these newcomers. She taught puppies the ropes and, while she wasn't all that partial to cats, she helped nudge kittens in the right direction. And, always, was that wagging plume of a tail. She smiled at everyone. Yes, really. She smiled. She lifted our spirits when we felt otherwise. Just watching that plume made us remember to focus on God's blessings and, standing right there in front of us, was one of His most rewarding.

Years passed and Smudge's health became severely compromised due to diabetes. She was placed on a strict eating regimen which meant the other dogs were required to adjust to her needs. I injected her with insulin twice each day. The vet stressed the need to keep the doses evenly spaced. I wondered, at first, how I'd manage. What if we went out for the evening and didn't return until midnight or later? What if . . . what if . . . what if? Then I looked down at that waving plume and asked myself how many times Smudge had placed parameters on her devotion to us. Never. We simply adjusted.

It was shortly after the diagnosis of diabetes that Smudge was faced with her next serious assignment. John was hit with a dizzy spell at just the wrong moment. He was about to begin navigating the stairs into my office when he lost his footing and careened to the landing, jamming one foot into the wall and bending the other one underneath him. Both ankles were shattered. After a lengthy stay at the emergency room, the orthopedic surgeon told him surgery would be risky due to his heart condition. His preference was for the ankles to heal on their own even though it would be a drawn-out process and, eventually, would result in an arthritic condition.

With casts and pain medication in place, we rented a walker and headed home. Smudge met us at the door. Neither of us understood how the little dog knew there was a problem, but she did.

Nursing John wasn't as easy for Smudge this time. The diabetes had begun taking its toll in earnest and one of those deep, kind eyes was ulcerated. I applied medication three times each day but nothing helped. The ulcer grew deeper and was obviously causing pain.

"Look at her," said the vet with a smile. "I know that eye's hurting her like blazes but her tail's still wagging."

"I know," I responded. It was hard to speak the next words but I somehow managed. "I know there's going to be an end to this," I choked out, "and I promised Smudge and me that I'd do what I had to when her tail stopped wagging."

The vet nodded, and cleared his voice. "The immediate problem is this eye. I don't see any alternative other than to remove it."

It sounded so extreme. "Can she handle that?" I asked.

Again, he smiled. "Can Smudge handle it? She can handle anything."

We set up the surgery appointment for the following day. They would do it in the morning. She could go home the following day if all went well, but I couldn't see her in-between. They wanted her to stay as still as possible, and my visiting could have the opposite effect.

The white tail was high and wagging as Smudge strutted into the office the next morning. The vet techs made over her and she reciprocated by making over them. I hugged her good-bye, and left without looking back.

Unfortunately, nothing could have prepared me for the way she would look the next time I saw her. I walked into the clinic the next afternoon, excited about fetching Smudge. The vet came out. "Diane," he said, "she looks much worse than she really is. There's a good deal more swelling than we antici-pated. Also, we felt we'd better put a collar on her because of all the stitches."

Just then Smudge came around the corner, pulling the tech toward the sound of my voice. I know everyone heard me suck in my breath. One side of the little dog's head was shaved. There was a long gash of black stitches stretching across a hor-ribly red and swollen lump of flesh. The "collar" was actually a very large, inverted, plastic "lampshade." I looked at her and felt the sobs welling up from somewhere deep down. Then the vet walked over and stood next to me, touching my arm.

"Look," he said. I followed his finger, pointing toward the plumed tail that was—what else?—wagging. I smiled and took hold of the leash. It was impossible to hug her around that lampshade but, then, I started laughing. This silly, little dog was actually prancing and making the lampshade look like a misplaced tutu! We went home.

Later that evening, while preparing dinner in the kitchen, I heard John's voice coming from the direction of the den. "Come on, Smudge. Move over."

Silence.

"Smudge, let me through."

Drying my hands, I started down the hall and burst into laughter as soon as I saw the cause of the one-sided conversation. There stood John, wobbling in his walker. And there stood Smudge, locked in unintentional combat with the metal legs that blocked the passage of her plastic lampshade. The two were in what appeared to be a hopeless tangle but, through it all, there was that wagging tail.

Smudge was six months or so past her thirteenth birthday. Her insulin dosage was being increased in steady and frequent increments. And her remaining eye was ulcerating. I kept watching her tail. It was my barometer, and I refused to admit it might be giving me a false reading.

I made an appointment with the vet and, after a cursory examination, he told me what I expected. "The other eye is going," he said in a flat voice, "and I really can't vouch for her overall quality of life. She may have another six months to a year but, again, I don't know how good the time will be."

"But you know I always said I'd do something when her tail stopped wagging," I almost whined.

He smiled slightly and shook his head. "I know, but look." He nodded toward the tail and, instantly, it began gently fanning the air. "I don't think it's ever going to stop. I just don't think you can use that as your signal."

I called John. "The only thing I know is I don't want her to suffer," he said. "She's been too good to us." I nodded into the receiver, knowing he couldn't see me.

"Oh, God," I thought, "this is hurting too much. Please help me to do this."

With tears already streaming down my face, I nodded in the affirmative to the vet. "Are you going to stay with her?" he asked. I nodded again. I couldn't speak.

I took her into the room. The vet and two attendants joined us. I knew the entire procedure would take only a few seconds, but I also knew there would be that one moment when she would begin feeling as if she couldn't breathe. I didn't want her to panic. I wanted to hold her head so her eye would look at me and she'd hear my voice. I wanted her life to leave her as gently as she'd lived it.

I began talking to her, and I didn't stop until I felt her body go limp and, just before that happened, her tail wagged one last time. Think what you will, I know that was Smudge telling me goodbye and not to worry because, after all, she would see me later.

Oh, Smudge taught us so much! She taught us that being happy is a choice as opposed to something that just happens. No, she wasn't human but she showed us how we could take what she had and transform it into a joy of the Lord that was always there, always wagging. Smudge had some bad, bad days but she never gave in to them. She chose to use what the Lord had given us. She showed me all the places where I fell short, but she also showed me how to just get up and do better the next time. It's called grace, and it comes from the Lord, and it is, truly, amazing.

And she taught us about mercy and forgiveness. And she reminded us over and over to be very careful about the way in which we entertain strangers lest we turn away or offend an angel of the Lord.

Smudge died but she didn't leave. We buried her in the yard and, even today, there are times when I see a plumed tail going around a doorway.

House Calls

KRISTIN VON KREISLER

Medusa, the dog of veterinarian Mark Esser, had an ominous name that evoked images of snakes for hair. She was also a Doberman pinscher, a breed that can terrify people. When visitors came to Esser's home in Sewell, New Jersey, they were often frightened when they heard her bark, and they froze, thinking that she would lunge at them through the front window.

When a new neighbor moved in across the street, Medusa trotted amiably over to meet him. She wagged her stump of a tail, panted a friendly welcome, and waited expectantly to be welcomed back.

"She's giving me the evil eye!" the neighbor shouted. "Is she going to bite?"

She'd only hoped that he would play with her, just as she played with the neighborhood children, Esser explained to the man. Every time she saw any of the children, she sniffed and nuzzled them. All she wanted was people's petting and affection.

Medusa was so loving that Esser sent her, like a roving therapist, to comfort people in distress.

One of them was a client, still distraught and crying all the time weeks after her dog had died from bone cancer. Daily, she carried her dog's ashes to her mailbox, so that he could "accompany" her as he'd done for many years. She refused to get another dog to ease her sadness. It could die, too, she insisted to Esser. She could never face such sorrow twice.

The woman needed grief counseling, but she was not likely to seek it out, and Esser, no psychologist himself, felt unqualified to help her. But Medusa could do it, he decided. Her sensitivity, which seemed to come so naturally, would have great healing power.

"Would you like for Medusa to visit you?" Esser asked the woman.

"All right," she agreed, but hesitantly.

Medusa bounded into her house as if she owned it. She plastered herself against the woman, who buried her face in Medusa's fur and cried. The dog, sensing that she was supposed to bring solace, stood, still and silent, beside the woman and let her pour out her sadness. Then Medusa nudged the woman's hand to ask for pets.

Medusa visited regularly for several months. Her comfort-dog therapy worked.

"Medusa got me through the roughest of times," the woman told Esser.

Her use of the past tense "got" showed that she had been healed.

Medusa also went to live with a man who was dying of lung cancer during his last month. She sat beside him and refused to leave except to eat or take a brief respite outdoors. When he grew too weak to get up from his chair, Medusa lay her head in his lap *for hours.* Finally, he had to go to the hospital, but Medusa stayed on to soothe his wife. Whenever she came home, sad from visiting her husband, Medusa was waiting for her with sympathetic whimpers.

No matter who needed comfort, Medusa, the "savage" Doberman, was there for them.

from THE COMPASSION OF ANIMALS

You Can Do It

"It matters not if you try and fail and try again. It matters much if you try and fail and fail to try again."

ANONYMOUS

Got any old dreams you gave up on? Running low on hope? Animals don't believe in such things. They believe in you, and your old dreams are very real to them. Let them persuade you to dust them off and go after them again. Only this time, take your animal friend along with you.

The Feisty Teacher

JOHN M. ALSTON

$\mathcal{W}$inter winds were still whipping western Montana well into the second week of April 1975. Throughout the long winter, I had entertained a dream of buying a registered malamute or Akita puppy in the spring. I visualized this finely bred puppy growing into a dog that would pull me up the rugged trails of the Selway-Bitterroot Wilderness while carrying his own food in a backpack.

I had lost both legs to a mortar shell while serving with the Marine Corps in Korea. This dream dog was to be my way of gaining access to the back country.

When I told my wife of my plans, she nodded and continued to work on a painting which she was completing, but that night at dinner she said, "You know, somebody will always be waiting in line to buy those expensive animals in the pet shops, but most of the puppies in the animal shelter will die." She said no more, but I began to rethink my dream. I had been left with no hope of living once; perhaps this memory gave me a deeper insight.

The next morning I drove to the Missoula Humane Society. "I need a special puppy," I told the young woman at the counter, "one that will be able to carry a heavy pack in the hills."

The woman's smile faded. "I'll show you the only puppy

we have left. Someone came in yesterday and left this little fellow. I fell in love with him; I tried to feed him, with no success, but there is something special about him."

Before I could tell her to forget it, she was through the door, and there I was in the cold waiting room wishing I had gone to the pet shop on the south side of town.

The woman returned with the saddest emaciated puppy I had ever seen. His tail was almost bare and hung like a winter twig. His head drooped and a tiny rib cage protruded through thin skin. His hide was pink where the hair was gone. I reached out and raised his head. He looked at me, but all hope was gone from his blue eyes. This was no vigorous sled dog to be sure, but I felt an instant rush of rapport with this deserted puppy. "I'll take him," I said.

"You'll take him?" the woman asked, beaming.

"Of course I'll take him," I answered, more composed now.

The woman brought out a paper, which I signed. "That will be ten dollars," she said, still smiling. She turned to the puppy, who could barely stand, and lifted his head and tail. "Hold up your tail," she whispered. "You've been adopted."

His tail remained slightly curled over his back as I carried him in my jacket to the station wagon. On the way home I massaged his ears gently and told him I expected great things of him, but he did not respond. When I got home, my wife met me at the door. "My goodness," she murmured, "he's pink."

"Oh, he's a little pink, all right," I admitted, "but look at those eyes. There's steel in those blue eyes." Little did I know.

After a few days of intensive care, those blue eyes did show a spark, and we named him Feist. For several days we thought Feist was retarded because he did not respond to any sounds; then one morning my wife had a hunch. "I believe Feist could be deaf," she said. She took him into the garage and blew a shrill whistle. Feist just sat on his blanket and looked at my wife with a vacant stare. He was totally deaf.

During the following six weeks Feist filled out and gained new strength. His tail became a bushy plume, which he wagged proudly. He seemed to like being outside even in the cold early spring, so I built him an insulated doghouse, lining it with blankets, which he promptly shredded. He ripped perennials from their beds, dug newly planted potatoes from their hills, and ravaged the strawberry bed. He even wrenched the lower limbs from small trees. My previous compassion began to wane. I became defensive. I fenced the garden, tied up what was left of the fruit trees, and nailed down a new mat in his house. I even thought of placing an ad in the local paper: "Beautiful Australian shepherd puppy—reasonable."

The last week of May arrived, and I was busy preparing and grading final exams, when the special education director for our school district called. "I'd like for you to come and visit some of my special education students," she said. "I think you might be an inspiration to them."

"What do you mean?" I asked. "How am I supposed to inspire special ed students?"

"You seem to have overcome your disability," she answered, "and you seem to walk rather well."

I was flattered. "Well, maybe I'll try to think of something. When is all this to take place and where do I go?"

"Could you be at Hawthorne School sometime Monday morning?"

"Monday morning, huh?" I mumbled.

"Oh, thank you so much," she said. There was a metallic click and silence.

All day Saturday and Sunday I wrote mini-speeches on scratch paper, crumpled them, and threw them in the trash. What could I possibly say to these young people with whom I had so little in common? I thought of my own trials, but I had never faced a problem of this nature from birth. I grew more uneasy.

I was still pondering my problem when my wife announced dinner. I was just sixteen hours away from making a fool of myself. As I passed the end of the table, a gray-blue blur shot past the patio door in hot pursuit of a low-flying bird. "That's it," I shouted. "I've got a deaf puppy, and he's overcoming his handicap with a vengeance."

I begged two other teachers to cover my morning classes, put a leash on a squirming Feist, and headed for Hawthorne School.

The halls were quiet when we arrived, but I found the special ed room easily.

We were greeted with "ooohs and aaahs" as Feist and I entered the room. I turned to greet one of the teachers when a small boy in a wheelchair tugged at my sleeve. "I'm going to die in a few weeks, you know," he said. I swallowed hard and looked back at Feist.

A little girl who had been lying on the floor tried to rise, but fell back. A thin boy who lay on a covered table strained to get a better look at Feist. My mind went blank. I looked down at Feist, who stood in the middle of the room looking from one wheelchair to another. *Why don't you just wag your tail,* I thought.

Suddenly, as if he had read my thoughts, Feist tilted his head to one side, raised his tail, wagged it several times, and leaped through the air into the lap of the boy who had said he was going to die. He licked the boy's face and pulled at his hair. The boy laughed until tears fell on his faded shirt. Feist whirled and bounded to the girl on the floor who had now raised herself to a sitting position. He knocked her flat and began tugging at her blouse the same way he had ripped out my strawberry plants. He darted and whirled from one child to another until the room was filled with laughing children and cavorting puppy. Abruptly he stopped at the doorway and wagged his tail as if to say, "Show's over, guys."

I still could think of nothing to say. I mumbled a thanks to the teachers for inviting us, but I was thinking of an old vaudeville saying: "Never follow a dog act."

Amid cheers, I led Feist toward the main entrance. There was one pillar in the center of the hall, and just as the young principal entered the hallway, Feist lifted his leg and sprinkled the column liberally. The principal stiffened, and I felt my face get hot, but behind us I heard a chorus of "Yea, Feist!"

Feist grew, in understanding as well as in stature. He learned to play ball and became a true athlete. When he leaped high for a long one, his body would arch through the air like a rainbow trout rising to a fly in the Bitterroot River. He learned that trees were not to be torn apart, that the forced air from heat ducts was not an invisible foe, that birds could not be caught in flight. But more important, he studied my every move and learned to adjust to my limitations. He would tilt his head to one side and study my gait, but he tested and challenged me always.

When I finally decided it was time for our first walk, I bought a new leash and braced myself.

He waited impatiently until I had a firm grasp on the leash, then he leaned into the collar like a sled dog on his first race.

I was launched into a half trot. I had not walked, if it could be called that, since Korea. I tried to slow him down, but he would have none of that. His trim legs churned and I lurched on in reluctant pursuit.

After nearly three weeks of this daily routine of at least a mile each day, I noticed that my breathing was easier and my legs were getting stronger. I began to look forward to our outings. Something akin to mild euphoria filled me for the first time in many years. I began to sniff the late spring air and enjoy the pungent smell of budding cottonwood. Sometimes Feist would pause to analyze some faint odor on the still morning air. There were times when we would take a break beside a stream; he would play at fishing for a floating leaf, looking back to see if I was watching his cavorting. The antics were not wasted. I learned to use new muscles by watching his graceful side-stepping. More important, I was now focusing more on him each day and less on myself. I began to realize that he was training me as a coach would prime an awkward child.

When we came to a deep stream, he would reconnoiter the bank and find a shallow place where I could cross, then splash to the other side, tail wagging furiously while I carefully chose the flattest rocks for footing. He showed me the easiest way around boulders and strained to pull me up steep inclines. He seemed to know my weaknesses, but he would tolerate no slacking on my part. If he was going to work at teaching, I would have to work at learning.

Feist accepted me as I was, but he challenged me to become my best self, to grow as he was growing, mentally and physically. Having no legs was no more an excuse for me than not hearing was an excuse for him.

For almost eighteen years, he showed indomitable courage. In his entire life he never once whined, whimpered, or complained in any way. He accepted life as it was, faced it squarely, and never backed away from anything or anyone.

Feist finally died in June of 1992, but he left behind a legacy: "Catch me if you can, and I'll teach you and be your shepherd." He is on the other side of the river now, tail wagging, eyes sparkling, beckoning to me to follow by treading on the deeply bedded rocks.

This is the true story of a remarkable dog who literally lifted my life several degrees. He was (and still is) an inspiration to me; because of his leadership, I still walk one and a half to two miles up and down hills each day. Feist is largely responsible for my present health and well-being.

I built a memorial to Feist in our backyard and my wife planted a flower garden around it. We give to the local animal shelter each month in his name so that other tails may wag and other people will learn.

We can't expect a perfect infant every time, but we can take what we are given and allow it to teach us to grow and blossom. This is what Feist taught.

from OUR BEST FRIENDS

Dinky: The Donkey That Loves Children

JOHN G. SUTTON

As a baby, Alexander Whelan-Archer was diagnosed as suffering from severe cerebral palsy, an illness that affects the central nervous system. He was also epileptic and had been born almost blind. The doctors said he would be lucky to live beyond the age of two. Refusing to believe that this baby boy would die so young, his adoptive mother Patsi devoted herself to caring for him. She had cared for children with special needs before, and thought that if she could just make little Alexander want to live, then he stood a chance.

Over the months Patsi tried everything to give this boy the will to survive. She hung the main room in her home with Christmas lights, wore a silly tinsel wig, sang to him, danced, and generally did all she could think of to stimulate Alexander. Then she had an idea. Near her home in Sutton Coldfield in the English Midlands, there is the Elisabeth Svendsen Trust center where disabled youngsters are given free rides on donkeys. Patsi thought that Alexander might respond to meeting one of these friendly creatures.

Patsi telephoned the center's manager, Sue Brennan, and told her about Alexander, who was now two years old. They were both invited to visit the next day. That night as Patsi prepared Alexander for bed, she told him that she had ridden a donkey once, one distant sunny day on the beach at Blackpool. Now it would be his turn.

Inside the EST center, Sue Brennan introduced Patsi and Alexander to the staff. Carrying Alexander in her arms, Patsi followed the staff instructors to an indoor enclosure. There stood a donkey called Dinky, already saddled up. He was all white with twinkling eyes and pointed ears. Patsi lifted Alexander up and one of the staff placed his tiny hands on Dinky's nose. Dinky gave a little wriggle of his head and for a second Alexander pulled back with a frightened look on his face. Being nearly blind, Alexander could not see the donkey but his sense of touch was extra sensitive. The animal must have felt strange and hairy to him. But after a moment he let the staff put his hands back on that funny, friendly head. This time he stroked one of Dinky's long ears. Patsi, who was still holding Alexander in her arms, could feel the joy running through him. His whole fragile little body seemed to tremble with pleasure and a wonderful smile lit up his face.

For the next six months Patsi took little Alexander to the EST center once a week. The boy loved every minute of it. The doctors at the hospital where he was born were astounded at how well and happy he was. Alexander was now all smiles and he tried his tiny best to control his limbs. The improvement in him so amazed the specialist in charge of Alexander's case that he asked if he could arrange an operation on the boy's eyes in an attempt to improve his vision.

Patsi will never forget the day she returned with her son to the EST center after his successful operation. Now little Alexander looked out at the world with beautiful clear green eyes. For the first time he could see his pal Dinky, and was able to ride without someone holding him.

Watching her child sitting on top of that donkey moved Patsi to tears. On the boy's face was a grin as wide as a mile. Alexander trotted round the arena laughing all the while as Dinky jogged him up and down. Patsi could see that despite all his terrible afflictions, her baby was, for once, gloriously happy.

Since that day Alexander has returned to the EST center at least once a week to see and ride his best friend Dinky the donkey. His treatment for cerebral palsy at a special school continues. This is helped along by the riding, which not only encourages the boy to use and control his muscles, but also brings great joy into his world.

By the age of six, Alexander had become one of the stars of the EST center. And much of his progress is thanks to a donkey called Dinky that just loves little children.

from ANIMALS MAKE YOU FEEL BETTER

The Nanny

DIANE M. CIARLONI

$\mathcal{I}$t was Sunday morning, and I knew I should get up if I wanted to arrive at church on time. It was, however, most definitely one of those "willing spirits but weak flesh" occasions. I decided to switch to the "just five more minutes" routine. I snuggled down into the pillow, surrounded by toasty warm dogs and cats, and began drifting immediately back to the ethereal world of dreams. Somewhere in the area of 17 seconds later, I was awakened by my husband.

"You better get up," he said.

"I know. I know. I'm going to be late for church."

"No," he said. "It's not that."

I raised up on one elbow, irritated by his intrusion. "Then what's the problem?" I demanded.

"We have company," he answered.

There was no way I could believe we had company at 8:30 on a Sunday morning. Surely we didn't know anyone who was that moronic.

"Come on. Get up," he instructed with a pronounced measurement of excitement. "I told her we'd be there in a few minutes. It's rude to leave her standing in the garage."

"I do not think this is a very funny game," I said tersely. "And I, for one, do not intend to continue playing it."

I attempted to turn over but, before I could complete the revolution, John jerked off the covers and grabbed my arm. "Come on!" he said.

"Okay. Okay. Let's get whatever this is over with so I can get dressed for church."

We went downstairs, through my office and into the garage which had one door open. There, sitting against a wall with about 20 pounds of flowing hair, was a collie. A very large collie. A very large sable-and-white collie with murl eyes which, I supposed, would have barred her from the show ring.

John squatted a few feet away from the dog, looking at her.

"I got into my very first fight over a collie," he said.

I arched one eyebrow into a question mark.

"I was walking home after school and I came to this guy who had a collie on the sidewalk, kicking and beating her as hard as he could. I jumped on him and started swinging."

"Did you win?" I asked.

"No, but the dog had enough time to get away. I never found out if she belonged to him or what, and I've never forgotten how awful it looked to see him doing that.

"Do you think that may be why this dog showed up?"

Oh, God! I didn't dare say yes. A collie? A very large collie in the house? My family raised collies when I was just a kid, and I knew they definitely were not intended as house dogs. This collie, however, since we did not have a fenced yard, would, by necessity, become a house guest. I wasn't sure I could handle it. My reaction was unusual since I'm the one who usually fights tooth and nail to keep an animal.

"Well," I said, "she's a beautiful dog and I think we should advertise. At least post notices at the vet clinic, animal shelter and run an ad in the local newspaper. If no one claims her—well—you should know collies aren't exactly the ideal house dogs."

"What should we name her?" he asked. It was as if everything I'd said sailed over the top of his head. "Lassie?"

I couldn't help it. Lassie? "Oh, please. No."

"Then what?" he countered.

I thought for a couple of seconds. "Sunday," I said. "She came here on a Sunday and (I glanced at my watch) she's made me too late to go to church."

Sunday it was.

It didn't take long to begin learning about the collie, and thus piecing together a plausible past. We found she'd been "debarked." What should have been a normal bark was nothing more than a very hoarse, semi-croak. That probably meant her previous owners lived in an apartment or condominium complex where noisy dogs were not tolerated.

Neither did it take long to figure out the dog had absolutely no idea of proper bathroom habits. Oh, she knew it was *verboten* to go inside but, somehow, someone had convinced her it was wrong to go *anywhere*. As a result, it wasn't unusual for her to last two or three or even four days without going to the bathroom—inside or outside. When she did go, however, she was most likely in one particular spot on a fairly expensive area rug in the living room. After a few drenchings, the rug smelled nothing less than horrible.

We also learned we had absolutely no hope of her going outside if we watched her. We needed to turn our backs—as in, very *obviously* turn our backs. There were times when I brought a hand mirror outside with me. That way, I could turn my back but still see. Sorta' like they do in beauty shops.

No one ever called to claim Sunday, so we just continued

fighting our battles with her. We needed more than one year to replace the house training inflicted on her by her original bungling owners, but it finally happened.

Sunday was just like the collies I remembered from more than 20 years earlier. Kind. Gentle. Self-sacrificing. The "Lassie" television series was on target. She was, in a pronounced way, timid and she couldn't tolerate or handle criticism in the form of discipline. The one or two times we tried it in regard to her bathroom habits, we stood and literally watched with our own eyes as her hair fell out in chunks! We never tried that again. The vacuum wasn't up to the stress.

Every animal in the house found an unwavering ally in Sunday. If we raised our voices at anyone, Sunday moved immediately between us and the offender. If we accidentally stepped on someone's tail and that someone squeaked, Sunday moved with the speed of light from wherever she was to wherever the other someone was. She sniffed the "injured" dog or cat from one end to the other, not resting until she was comfortable regarding the animal's welfare.

I soon lost track of how many hours the collie spent stretched out on the floor, remaining motionless while a cat spent 20 minutes kneading her belly. Or she would bathe a bunny until its hair was soaking wet. There's never a dirty eye in the house because Sunday makes the rounds daily, licking away anything that shouldn't be there. She lets others eat before she does, standing back and waiting. She never pushes in for treats, but makes certain everyone else has enjoyed the tasty morsel.

She's the same way with people, especially children, as she is with animals. She's a born nanny, no references required. I sometimes listen to the child-care horror reports and think everyone should have a Sunday. Little ones can lie across her back, or put a blanket on the floor and go to sleep with their arms around the big dog. I look at her and remember a collie from my past named Gidget. We frequently put small cousins in the yard and gave Gidget "instructions" as to where they could and could not go. She always understood. No one was allowed in the driveway. If they tried, Gidget moved in front of the diminutive body and gently but persistently pushed him back toward the yard. Sunday is the same way.

Sunday isn't an easy dog to have. She sheds horribly, and it's difficult to control the odor. There are many times when I find myself wishing someone had called about the big collie, excited about finding their dog. On the other hand, I felt relatively certain Sunday was a dump-off. Why did she just show up like that? Her paws didn't show a lot of wear and tear, so I knew she hadn't travelled a great distance on foot to reach us. She was wearing no collar, no tags. So the likelihood of anyone becoming excited about finding their dog was very remote. Even with those occasional musings, I'm grateful for all Sunday has given. She's 12 now and she's helped raise numerous cats, dogs and rabbits. She's devoted countless hours to bathing and grooming and babysitting.

It's becoming more difficult for the big collie to perform her nanny duties. She's arthritic in her hind quarters, making it difficult for her to get up and down. Navigating the stairs is now a chore but, while she may be a bit slower, she continues handling her many responsibilities.

Any animal who has been a member of a family for several years teaches its own special lessons. Sunday is no exception.

The big, long-haired collie is the sublime illustration of Dale Carnegie when he said, "You can make more friends in two months by becoming more interested in other people than you can in two years by trying to get people interested in you."

And so it is with Sunday. No thoughts of herself, with her entire concentration centered on someone else.

Buying Blind

CAROL FLEISCHMAN

Have you ever tried to buy a dress when you can't see? I have, because I'm blind. At one time, I would shop with friends. This ritual ended after an incident which showed me that I needed to be more discriminating about their tastes. Happily bringing home a dress which a friend helped me choose, my husband, Don, offered a surprising observation: "The fit is great, but do you like all those huge fish?" The dress went back.

Now I rely on Don and my guide dog Misty as my shopping partners. We enter the store and make a beeline for the dress department. Don sees two or three salespeople scatter. The aisles empty, as if a bomber is on the scene. Then I realize I'm holding the "live wire." I'm not judgmental, once I, too, was uneasy around large dogs. Although Misty is better behaved than most children, I know a 65-pound German Shepherd is imposing.

On one recent shopping trip, a brave saleswoman approached us. "Can I help you?" she said to my husband.

"Yes, I'm looking for a dress," I replied (since I will wear it, not him). "Maybe something in red or white."

"RED OR WHITE," she said, very slow and loud (though my hearing is fine). I managed not to fall as Misty jumped back on my feet, frightened by the woman's booming voice. Don was distracted, too. I heard him rustling through hangers on a nearby rack. I called his name softly to get his attention. Another man answered my call. What were the chances of two Dons being within earshot?

"This is great!" Don said holding up a treasure. I swept my hand over the dress to examine it. It had a neckline that plunged to the hemline. "Hmm"—I walk three miles daily with Misty, and stay current with fashion, but I'm positive this costume would look best on one of the Spice Girls.

Finally, I chose three dresses to try on. Another shopper distracted Misty, even though the harness sign reads: "Please do not pet. I'm working." She said, "Your dog reminds me of my Max, who I recently put to sleep," so I am sympathetic. We discuss her loss for 15 minutes (some therapists don't spend that much time with grieving clients).

Don was back. He told me the route to travel to the dressing room. I commanded Misty: right, left, right and straight ahead. We wove our way past several small voices: "Mom, why is that dog in the store?" "Mom, is that a dog or a wolf?" My personal favorite is: "But that lady's eyes are open." I trust these parents to explain: "The lady is giving her guide dog commands. Her dog is a helping dog. They're partners." I questioned whether this positive message has been communicated when I heard an adult say: "Oh, there's one of those blind dogs."

Other people, though well-intentioned, can interfere with my effective use of Misty. Guide dogs are highly trained and very dependable, but occasionally make potentially dangerous mistakes. On my way through the aisles, Misty bumped me into a pointed rack, requiring my quick action. I used a firm tone to correct her, and she dived to the ground like a dying actress. Witnessing this performance, another shopper chastised me for being cruel. I was shocked. Misty's pride was hurt, but I needed to point out the error in order to avoid future mistakes. If I did not discipline her, what would prevent Misty from walking me off the curb into traffic?

Composing myself, I was delighted by the salesperson's suggestion: "Can I take you to your dressing room?" I was less delighted when she grabbed me and pushed me ahead while Misty trailed us on a leash. I wriggled out of the woman's wrestling hold. Gently pushing her ahead, I lightly held her elbow in sighted guide technique (called so because the person who sees goes first).

"This is better. Please put my hand on the door knob. I'll take it from there," I said. In the room, Misty plopped down and sighed with boredom. I sighed with relief that she was still with me. Once I was so preoccupied with trying on clothes that Misty sneaked out beneath the dressing room doors. I heard her tags jingling as she left, but was half-dressed and couldn't retrieve her. Fortunately, Don was outside the door and snagged her leash.

I modeled the dresses for Don and, feeling numb, bought all three. Leaving the store, Misty's magnetism, like the Pied Piper, attracted a toddler who draped himself over her. She remained calm as he tried to ride her. The boy's fun was soon foiled by his frantic mother.

When we returned to our car, I gave Misty a treat and lots of praise. A good day's work deserves a good day's pay for both of us. "Shop till you drop" or "retail therapy" could never be my motto. To me, "charge" means going into battle.

Something to Bark About

CHRISTINE A. VERSTRAETE

---

*H*er gait is a little slower now, her step not as sprightly. Her ears still are alert, though, and as morning breaks, she listens for any sound of movement from behind the bedroom door.

She trots steadily down the hall, pausing outside that particular door to listen for a thump or any other sound. The door opens, a wheelchair slowly enters the hall and Roxy stands alert, her tail wagging excitedly as she falls into her place at the side of the disabled boy.

The bond that Roxy, a 13-year-old yellow Labrador Retriever, shares with Stuart Rabin, a 14-year-old with severe cognitive disabilities, has developed naturally.

Roxy is not a trained service dog. She wasn't even trained as a therapy dog. She is, simply, a dog with a big heart and a special gift.

"They've got a special relationship," says Stuart's mother, Anne. "The dog knows when there's something wrong with Stuart. She is a very calming influence to him. She's totally a part of his world."

Stuart was 10 months old when Anne and her husband, Jerry, who at the time lived in Waukegan, Ill., realized their first child was not developing as he should. They wondered, worried and finally went to see a doctor. At first they got conflicting reports, diagnoses and misdiagnoses. It wasn't until Stuart was around age 7 that they learned their son had Angelman's syndrome. Caused by a deletion on a chromosome, the syndrome results in learning disabilities, a still, jerky gait, inability to speak, seizures and sleep disorders.

Even though Anne, who grew up in a frequently moving military family, had never owned a dog, the idea of getting one seemed comforting in that time of sorrow.

"Stuart was 3, he wasn't getting better and there wasn't a miracle cure for him," she recalls. "I got it in my mind that I'd like to get a dog."

Anne was drawn to Labrador Retrievers based on her research, her brother's experiences with the breed, recommendations from friends and the breed's reputation for having a gentle disposition. Training and working with Roxy became therapeutic for her as well. "It was very healing to me," she says.

Roxy's disposition turned out to be gentle and more. Even when Roxy was younger she seemed to have a special understanding for Stuart's frailties and limitations. The dog sat next to him. He crawled, and the dog was right there. "He was on the floor, she was right next to him," Anne says. "She used to lie next to him. When he was eating, she'd be right next to his high chair."

Most of all, Anne saw that Roxy motivated the boy. "She helped him by making him pay attention," Anne explains. "He couldn't sit up for years and years. Having Roxy there, she was constantly giving him attention, rubbing him. It kind of made him get up to a prone position, then sit up . . . "

Roxy showed that same instinctive concern and caring

nature when she visited Stuart's class. The dog would be just as gentle, solicitous and caring about other children with disabilities.

This past February, Roxy was recognized for her contributions and her relationship to the Rabin family of Pleasant Prairie, Wis., by being named Companion Pet of the Year in the Wisconsin Veterinary Medical Association's Pet Hall of Fame. In its sixth year, the annual awards program honors pets for their contributions in the Hero, Professional and Companion categories.

Roxy was nominated for her role in Stuart's life by her veterinarian, Dr. William Carlisle, who's been with the Kenosha Animal Hospital in Kenosha, Wis., for 20 years. He says he was surprised but gratified to learn of Roxy being chosen as the winner, considering the hundreds of entries submitted to the contest each year.

It also was the first time he'd nominated a dog. "A lot of it was primarily the relationship I saw, the bond Roxy had with her owner and just hearing the story of her relationship with Stuart," Carlisle says.

He also could see the commitment the Rabins had to helping Roxy, who they brought to Carlisle two years ago suffering with severe osteoarthritis. "It was in all her joints, and her quality of life was failing," he says. "They weren't ready to say goodbye, and they certainly didn't want Roxy to suffer."

"She was so miserable," Anne recalls. "She didn't want to socialize. She was just taking herself off to her corner. I was pretty sure she was dying. Other vets kept telling us she's old. I just kept feeling there's something we can do. There's no reason she should be in such discomfort."

Carlisle performed surgery on both of Roxy's knees. The

dog now receives monthly injections and takes at least seven kinds of medications.

Easing Roxy's pain didn't come cheaply, but Anne says seeing the dog more comfortable and back to pretty much her old self was worth every penny. "She's my million-dollar dog," Anne jokes. "It's expensive, but she's worth it."

Stuart now attends special education classes at the middle school and is scheduled to enter high school next year.

While Roxy has taught their son to persevere, Anne says that she also learned a lot from Roxy.

"The best thing about having Roxy, besides the relationship and companionship we have, is how she taught me to have a lot of patience," Anne says. "In teaching her and working with her, a lot of those skills were similar skills I'd use in working with my son. She helped me to teach her things and not get discouraged, to persevere."

Although Roxy now is doing as well as can be expected given her age, Anne says she tries not to look too much forward.

The family does have a second dog, Corky, a 7-year-old female German Shepherd Dog. Anne says, however, that she's not sure how Stuart would react to Roxy no longer being there.

For now, it's like being given extra minutes on the clock— precious minutes. "She's just really super," Anne says. "She's really, really precious to us. Now she's fine. She walks slowly, but her tail's wagging."

from DOG WORLD

Charlie, the Arctic Explorer

KAREN DERRICO

$\mathcal{A}$t the age of sixty-one, Helen Thayer has fulfilled many of her lifelong dreams of adventure. At fifty-six, she kayaked and walked 1,200 miles through the Amazon. And a few years ago she recently finished walking 1,400 miles across the Sahara Desert. But one of Helen's most amazing and memorable adventures to date was her solo trek to the magnetic North Pole in 1988, at the age of fifty.

After many years of mountaineering, including climbing the highest peaks in North and South America and the Soviet Union, Helen decided the time had come for a new challenge. After two years of preparation and planning, she set out to become the first woman to travel by ski and foot alone to the North Pole.

Three days before her departure, she made a last-minute decision to adopt a black husky and Newfoundland mix to accompany her on the expedition. She purchased the dog from an Inuit who used him and other sled dogs as tools and not as pets. Like most sled dogs, this dog had no name, was fed frozen seal meat twice a week, and chewed ice for water.

Helen named her dog Charlie and together they set off on a

grueling 27-day, 365-mile journey to the magnetic North Pole. They faced fierce wind and weather, with wind chill temperatures dropping to one hundred degrees below zero. They trekked across breaking sea ice that tilted under their feet, and howling arctic storms that blew their food and equipment into oblivion. At one point, Helen's eyelids froze shut, and one eye was seriously injured.

The brave duo lived through many exciting adventures as well as frightening encounters with polar bears. Charlie had been specially trained to alert humans to polar bears and saved Helen's life many times during their trip. She credits much of her survival and perseverance to the intimate relationship between her and Charlie. When they were just seven days away from reaching the North Pole, a storm destroyed Helen's food supply and fuel for melting ice to drink. Although she was starving, she refused to take any of Charlie's remaining dog food for herself. On April 27, 1988, Helen and Charlie finally reached their destination, making them the first solo dog and woman team to ever reach the North Pole.

At journey's end, Charlie returned with Helen to her home in Snohomish, Washington. There he was introduced to a brand new world of grass, trees, flowers, and rain, in addition to Helen's three other dogs, five goats, two donkeys, and one cat. Not only did the once nameless dog now have a name, but he had a loving family and home for the first time in his life. Helen chronicled her amazing adventure with Charlie in the best-selling book *Polar Dream.*

With sled dog days far behind him, Charlie enjoys daily ten-mile jogs with Helen and her husband Bill, and also accompanies them on mountain climbs, hikes, and ski trips. Charlie is between twelve and fourteen years old, but as Helen says,

"He's as fit as a six- or seven-year-old dog." She prepares daily home-cooked meals for Charlie and her other dogs and takes Charlie once a month to the chiropractor and acupuncturist. Together with Helen, Charlie makes regular visits to local schools where he circulates through the crowd offering kisses and a wagging tail.

from UNFORGETTABLE MUTTS

Urban Encounters

TONI EAMES

I ncorporating animals into our lives as family members usually results in new and exciting experiences. For me, sharing life with a guide dog has expanded my world in many ways.

I completed training with my first guide dog, a Golden Retriever named Charm, just before entering graduate school at Hunter College in Manhattan. During that first semester, Jerry, a dog lover, sat next to me in several classes. During class break, I would permit Jerry and other students to pet Charm while she maintained her Sit Stay. Jerry, in particular, was an enthusiastic admirer and got in more than his fair share of strokes. After a couple of weeks he confessed he was having difficulty explaining to his suspicious wife why he returned from school with long blonde hair on his jacket. She poohpoohed his claim that the hair belonged to his classmate's dog! Several weeks later, when his wife attended class with Jerry, she exclaimed with relief, "There really is a blonde dog in class!"

On the way home from school, I needed to negotiate through a pack of loud, hoodlum-like teenagers hanging out at a corner candy store. Approaching them with trepidation, I came up with a brilliant idea. As I worked my way through the milling throng, I called out, "Watch it, guys, new driver!"

The guys thought that was funny and asked if I needed

help crossing the street. Actually, the street was more the size of an alley and I was able to hear a car coming two blocks away, but not wanting to antagonize them, I graciously accepted their offer and told them to let me know when it was safe to cross! That ploy worked so well, whenever I used that route home I could count on getting help. In fact, I had the feeling that if I were bothered by anyone after going by, these gang members would come to my rescue!

When Ed joined me many years later, he told me about a peculiar experience he had walking home from the subway. A bunch of boisterous teenagers outside a local hangout stopped their antics and told him when it was safe to cross. He was bewildered by this offer of help, because the street he was crossing was such a quiet and safe one! Victoriously, I explained how I converted these potential thugs into allies!

Like most young unmarried women of my generation, I wanted to meet someone, fall in love and get married. For a blind woman, this process is more difficult. At one point I resorted to a dating service, "Single Pet Lovers," and got to meet a young man I liked. After a few minutes in my apartment where I introduced him to guide dog, Flicka, and cats, Disney and Tevye, we went off to have dinner at my favorite diner. As we took the 15-minute walk, conversation flowed easily, much of it related to pets.

On entering the lobby of the Flagship Diner, without warning, Flicka threw up. One of the hostesses who knew us ran over and said this was the first time anything like that had ever happened. She called a bus boy to clean up the mess and led us to our table. Although my new acquaintance did not seem shaken by the incident, and dinner went well, he never called me after that! Over the next few weeks, my disappointment gave way to recognition that the potential romance would never have blossomed. With a house full of animals, a man who couldn't deal with a little vomit would never have made it as my mate.

1970, when I started working at Kings Park Psychiatric Center, commuting on the Long Island Rail Road became part of my everyday life. This frequently entailed long waits during freezing weather, trains not showing or arriving more than an hour late, sitting in cars where the heat or air-conditioning was not working, etc. However, one of the worst problems resulted from careless fellow passengers who spilled their coffee or other drinks on the floor. This invariably meant my guide dog would end up with these liquids imbedded in her fur and have to go through an extensive cleaning process.

One day, as I boarded the train on my way home from work, I found a particularly nasty pool of spilled sugary coffee on the floor. My dander was up and I rebelled! Instead of insisting that Flicka lie down in that puddle of muck, I told her to get on the empty seat next to me. When the conductor came along to collect tickets, he demanded I remove the dog from the seat. I told him that if he found a seat for me where my dog could lie on the floor without getting dirty, I'd be glad to move. He was furious, but moved on muttering under his breath.

After a couple of stops, the train filled up and a few men were standing around chatting about their day at work. The conductor saw this as a golden opportunity to dislodge Flicka from her unauthorized seat. Approaching the group of standees, he asked them if they would like a seat. They declined saying they were comfortable standing. The disgruntled conductor's next move in this charade was to call two security guards to dislodge Flicka from her perch. They were horrified when I pointed out the congealed glop of spilled coffee on the floor and said they couldn't blame me for not wanting my dog lying down in that mess. They then inquired of the standing passengers whether anyone wanted Flicka's seat, and they all declined the offer. Turning to the conductor, who stood by glaring, they asked him what the problem was. During the entire trip, Flicka lay on the seat with her head in my lap.

After all this commotion, I heard my station being announced and sighed with relief. As Flicka and I stepped off the train, I turned around to the standing passengers and security guards, and called out, "Thanks, guys!" Fortunately, I never ran into that conductor again!

Several years after joining the staff at KPPC, a fellow worker came to my office with a wonderful request. Sister Dorothy Dengel had recently moved into a new convent where she was not permitted to have a dog. Without a dog of her own, she asked if she could play ball with Flicka on the lawn outside the back door near my office. I was delighted with the offer, and every morning during the coffee break, rain, snow or shine, Sister Dorothy came for Flicka and the two of them headed outside for some well-deserved recreation. Flicka quickly learned to anticipate Sister Dorothy's arrival and would be waiting at the door, tennis ball in mouth.

As Sister Dorothy and I began exchanging views about the world, and particularly the place of animals in that world, our friendship flourished. Periodically on Fridays she would come home with me to spend the night so we could attend an anti-fur rally in Manhattan the following day. After such an event, however, our varying personalities emerged. I would go home and call all my friends to share the experience with them. She, on the other hand, would go back to Long Island and spend the rest of the weekend contemplating the event and internalizing all her feelings.

When Flicka was diagnosed with cancer at the age of seven, Sister Dorothy became my main emotional support. Faced with occasional crises during Flicka's treatment, Sister Dorothy took time out of her busy schedule to take us to the veterinary hospital. As the end approached, I knew Flicka's death would have almost as heavy an impact on her as it would on me. In my grief, I wrote about the devastation Flicka's pending death was bringing into the lives of those who loved her and me:

"Friends are very important at a time like this. The pain is incredibly intense. Knowing many people care, letting me know they are within reach of a telephone or a hug, really helps. Oh, thank you, dearest friends, it helps! Flicka is so well-loved, so vital, so joyous, her pending death is a wrench and a heart-shredding pain to her many fans.

"What about Sister Dorothy's grief? She had become Flicka's godmother shortly after Flicka came into my life. My beloved guide adores her and, in her moments of deepest lethargy on this dreadful, life-prolonging medication, Flicka will rally for a run with Dorothy. I witness the devastating blow Flicka's illness has dealt this gentle, loving woman and, again, I feel so helpless!"

As soon as Flicka's successor, Ivy, arrived on the scene, she was incorporated into the play routine. Following Flicka's lead, Ivy quickly came to adore this gentle devoted nun. Following Flicka's death, Ivy gained Sister Dorothy's undivided attention, and their love for each other knew no bounds.

Shortly after our move to Fresno, Sister Dorothy temporarily conquered her fear of flying and took the only airplane trip in her life to visit us. Several years later, we reciprocated by spending a few days with her in her Queens apartment. When we got off the train at the elevated station near where she lived, Ivy, spotting Sister Dorothy at the other end of the platform, almost jumped out of her harness to greet her. Ed's guide Kirby, who had never met Sister Dorothy, picked up on Ivy's excitement and began dragging Ed down the platform!

For the next few days, both dogs got to play with Sister Dorothy in her fenced-in backyard. It was wonderful seeing this quiet and reclusive friend come to life in the presence of our two cavorting dogs!

Lessons in Kitty-Speak

LYNN SEELY

$\mathcal{I}$ looked at the quarter-mile track and sighed. The white lane-lines were freshly painted and seemed to mock me. Surely they were there for real runners, not someone like me. I had recently undergone back surgery, and the asphalt oval that loomed before me seemed like an almost impossible distance to navigate. My intention had been to start out walking on the track, then attempt to run slowly for a short distance. My resolve wavered for a moment. Maybe I should reconsider. Maybe I should wait and try this another day.

"Meooowwww mmmurrrrrrr!"

I looked down at the source of the comment and smiled. Mesha, my tiny companion, was looking up at me expectantly. She has always been a talkative cat and today was no exception. I made up my mind that I'd try to exercise this morning. After all, I didn't want to disappoint Mesha.

Mesha is of questionable Siamese extraction, and although she is getting on in years, she still seems as spry as ever. Only the fur on one of her back paws shows a tell-tale sign she is aging, for the once-dark-velvet-brown color has faded to a pale gray. Yet her blue eyes are still bright, she still plays like a kitten every night, and she is as vocal as ever, commenting when it suits her upon anything she deems important. And, as it happens, many things seem important to Mesha.

Her frequently expressed opinions are in effusive kitty-speak, and I am convinced she believes I should understand every single word she meows. In fact, she seems mystified if I don't grasp her meaning. When that happens, she will repeat herself in yowling kitty-speak, getting progressively louder and louder until she makes me understand—or until she gets so exasperated she falls silent.

Though her pedigree may be in question, her loyalty, love and sweet temperament are not. She proved that during the time I was in excruciating pain before back surgery, and again when I had to endure weeks of painful rehabilitation. Part of the rehabilitation included being prone on my sofa for hours each day while I was in traction. This went on day after day, week after week. And every day, during those long hours, little Mesha was my constant, caring companion.

Each day, after I was settled on the sofa, she would carefully climb onto my stomach, then lie down facing me. After tucking her petite brown paws neatly under her slender body she would gaze intently at my face for long periods of time. If she saw tears rolling down my face, due to the pain I was in, she would stretch out one dainty paw toward my cheek in a tender gesture of comfort, then try to console me with her expressive kitty-speak meows. Day after day this was repeated. I would cry, then she would reach out her delicate paw and kitty-speak. She would then pause, waiting quietly for me to unburden myself. I would stroke her silky fur and tell her my troubles as she listened attentively. Sometimes the expression on her face was so clearly perplexed, her little brow was wrinkled with such worry, and her gaze was so clearly concerned that I found myself smiling even as tears poured down my face.

I would then reassure her I was going to be okay—though at times I admit I had my doubts.

We used to be carefree and have great fun before this. Mesha used to enjoy watching me hit the tiny square things on my keyboard as we both sat close to my computer; she on top and I in front. And she took great delight in bursting the silence with one boisterous, kitty-speak "MEEEEOOWWWHH" every so often. It was her task to startle me and my role to jump, and we both did our parts well.

Mesha used to adore going for a ride in my car when I had errands to do and she loved going on walks with me. And sometimes, during the walk, we'd run together just for fun. She had her very own special harness and leash, as well as a pretty blue collar that matched the deep cerulean of her eyes. Whenever she wanted to go outside with me she would go to the cabinet and stare pointedly at the drawer where they were kept. If I didn't notice her immediately, she would begin her chorus of kitty-speak, the volume rising steadily until I responded. But since I had been injured, she had not shown any interest in going anywhere or doing any of the things we once did. I believe she thought it was her loving duty to keep me company, a duty she did willingly.

Time is a great healer of the body and as the days went by my tears were more infrequent as the pain diminished. I was getting better. And as I got better, Mesha decided I needed to be doing more than just resting all the time. I was still reluctant to walk more than a few steps, but Mesha seemed to understand that it was time to get me moving again. And she contrived a simple yet unique solution that was guaranteed to make me start exercising.

One morning Mesha put her plan into action. Instead of

joining me where I lay on the sofa, Mesha walked through the living room, glanced meaningfully in my direction, then headed toward the back porch. Once there, she started calling me. "Meooowhaa Murhhh." Which meant "Oh-do-come-look-at-this!" in kitty-speak. I answered by calling her to me. I did not want to get up and attempt to walk to where she was.

The house was silent for a moment. Then she called me again in a more insistent voice. "Maeeooooowwwhwwwwhh!" she said loudly. I knew that tone. It was "I-said-to-come-HERE," in kitty-speak. I still wasn't about to get up and so I called her again. "I don't want to get up Mesha, so come back here, sweetie, and rest with me."

Mesha, however, has a stubborn streak. And she wasn't about to give in, no matter how pleasantly I spoke to her. A moment later she started to call me again, and this time she pulled out all the stops! Let me tell you something: a full-volume Siamese caterwaul is not a sound any hearing individual can ignore for long!

"MMMMMMMOOOOOOOWWWUUUUURRRRRRHH!" Mesha's long, piercing, emphatic yowl, equivalent to the banshee wail of a bagpipe being stomped on by an elephant—a very large elephant—couldn't have been more disconcerting! It was impossible to ignore.

I could stand it no longer! She clearly wanted me to come to where she was. "Oh, all right, Mesha," I grumbled to her. "I'll come out." Hearing that, Mesha suddenly fell silent. I got up slowly, wrapped my old bathrobe about me and took small, tentative steps as I made my way cautiously toward her. She stared up at me as I entered the room. "Meeeoooowwh-muuhhh," she said in soft-kitty-speak. That translated roughly into "I'm-so-glad-to-see-you-but-it's-about-time." Her blue eyes had a gleeful look in them. My annoyance quickly changed to mirth. How could I possibly stay annoyed at Mesha?

I sat down in a chair and Mesha immediately jumped up onto my lap. She chortled to me happily as she settled down. I had forgotten how much I loved being in this room. It had always been a special place, a comfort to me. My back porch is a lovely, bright room built with large windows on three sides. Sunlight streams in each morning and warms the two cozy over-stuffed chairs that face the windows. From here, I have a splendid view of the mountain and woods, and there is usually some type of wildlife within view. Yet I had not ventured out here in many months. The living-room sofa was an easier walk from my bedroom and until Mesha intervened, I had no intention of walking farther than I had to.

She was now on a mission, it seemed, for the next day she wanted to take a walk down to the mailbox. She stood by the cabinet that held her leash and harness and stared at me. "Meeooouuuuhhhh?"

I decided I would take a little walk with her. How could I say no? After all, how could I disappoint her after she had been so devoted to me? I put the pretty blue collar and harness on her, then attached the leash.

Off we went down the driveway, which is over 300 feet long, and it has a fairly steep grade to it. Going down was easier than I had imagined it would be, but the walk back was extremely tiring. I had to stop and rest often. Each time I stopped, Mesha would stand by my side, her long elegant tail swaying gently back and forth as she patiently waited for me to recover. She spoke to me in kitty-speak each time we stopped and I wondered if perhaps she was trying to encourage me to keep going.

As if she read my mind the moment I entertained such an idea, she loudly proclaimed an emphatic "Muuurrroooohhh!" We finally made it back to the house and though I was tired, my spirits were lifted. After I removed her harness I collapsed onto the sofa. I was tired yet pleased at the progress I was making. Mesha jumped up to where I was, then gave me a sweet kiss on the tip of my nose as she did when she wanted to express great affection. She then added a comment: "Mmmmuuurrrrrrhhhh!" I'm sure that meant "Congratulations!" in kitty-speak.

Each day the same walk was repeated, and each day I was able to stay off the sofa for longer periods of time. As I grew stronger, Mesha wanted to do more activities. One day she decided it was time for a car ride. She explained in loud kitty-speak that the walk up and down the driveway wasn't enough. We had just returned to the house from a walk when she went over to my purse and started pawing at it. I wondered what she was doing. I should have known, as she had done this sort of thing before. After a few minutes of thrusting her paws into the depths of the purse, she pulled out her prize, my car keys. She then looked at me and yowled as if her heart would break. I knew exactly what she had on her mind. She wanted to go "bye-bye." I sighed, then picked up the keys. "Okay, Mesha, we'll go bye-bye, but just a short distance." It had been a very long time since I had driven a car. Perhaps Mesha was right. Perhaps today was a good day to go on a short drive.

I carried Mesha to the car and we got in. I had to admit it was an excellent idea, after all. As I drove down the driveway, I noticed Mesha looked perfectly pleased with herself as she curled up on the seat next to me. Her objective had been achieved. We were going for a drive. It was wonderful to be able to do this again and I thoroughly enjoyed it. So did Mesha.

This "bye-bye" routine repeated itself often over the next few weeks. With all the exercise I was now getting, the idea started to form in my mind that maybe, just maybe, I could start running again sometime. Which brings me back to the start of this story, back to the morning Mesha and I were standing on the track.

It was time to begin. Time to try. I took a deep breath and said, "Okay, Mesha, I'm ready if you are." Mesha peered intently into my eyes, then replied, "Murrr-oeooo! Mewouhha! Maahhhh!" I knew exactly what she had just spoken in kitty-speak: she was ready to start.

I began walking slowly in my lane. Mesha started walking in the lane next to me. Mesha has been on many adventures with me and this was just one more as far as she was concerned. Nothing odd here. It seemed perfectly natural to her that she should be walking next to her human companion on a deserted high-school track. I was so focused on watching Mesha that I forgot for a moment how impossible this very act of walking had seemed not too long ago. I was soon ready to attempt a few minutes of running.

"Come on, Mesha, let's go faster." I started to run slowly and Mesha began trotting along in the lane next to me. She apparently had no intention of stopping. She seemed to be having a great time and I found myself laughing and talking to her as she trotted along next to me. She never strayed into my lane and every once in a while she would glance up at me and add her kitty-speak-comments. I made it around the track once that day with Mesha, walking most of the time and running slowly a few times.

Since then, I've been able to compete in many running

events, including two marathons. And after each one, as soon
as I get home, I scoop Mesha up in my arms and tell her how
much I missed her. She always answers, "MMUURRHHMM,"
which means, in kitty-speak, "I missed you, too."

ACKNOWLEDGMENTS
(continued from page ii)

"The Power of Pets," by Micki Siegel, is from *Good Housekeeping,* November 1995.

"Just My Dog" is from *Tears & Laughter,* by Gene Hill. Copyright © 1981 by Gene Hill. Published by Countrysport Press.

"Purr-fect Pals for Sick Kids" and "Omar Khayyam," by Roberta Sandler, are used by permission of the author.

"Our Guard(ian) Dog," by Elizabeth Polk, is from *Angels on Earth,* May/June 2000.

"To Smell a Rat" is from *Emergency Vet,* by Lillian M. Roberts. Copyright © 1998 by Lillian M. Roberts. Published by The Ballantine Publishing Group.

"Coco, My Little Hero," by Anne Watkins, is used by permission of the author.

"A Cat With a Nose for Danger," by Donna Boetig, is from *McCall's,* February 1998.

"The Warning," by Patrick Flanagan and Gael Crystal Flanagan, is from *Animal Miracles,* by Brad Steiger and Sherry Hansen Steiger. Copyright © 1999 by Brad Steiger and Sherry Hansen Steiger. Published by Adams Media Corporation.

"Betty Boop and the Gang" is from *The Dog Who Rescues Cats,* by Philip Gonzalez and Leonore Fleischer. Copyright © 1995 by Philip Gonzalez. Published by HarperCollins Publishers, Inc.

"Greta, My Guardian Pony," by Thirza Peevey, is used by permission of the author.

"Nurse Smudge" and "The Nanny," by Diane M. Ciarloni, are used by permission of the author.

"The Feisty Teacher," by John M. Alston, is from *Our Best Friends,* by Michael Capuzzo and Teresa Banik Capuzzo. Copyright © 1998 by Michael Capuzzo and Teresa Banik Capuzzo. Published by Bantam Books, a division of Bantam Doubleday Dell Publishing Group, Inc.

"Dinky: The Donkey That Loves Children" is from *Animals Make You Feel Better,* by John G. Sutton. Copyright © 1998 by John G. Sutton. Published by Element Books, Inc.

"Buying Blind," by Carol Fleischman, is used by permission of the author.

"Something to Bark About," by Christine A. Verstraete, is from DOGWORLD, August 2000.

"Charlie, the Arctic Explorer," is from *Unforgettable Mutts,* by Karen Derrico. Copyright © 1999 by Karen Derrico. Published by NewSage Press.

"Urban Encounters," by Toni Eames, is used by permission of the author.

AN INVITATION TO OUR READERS

If you would like to share a true story about an animal in your life, we invite you to send it to us. If you would like more information about the *LISTENING TO THE ANIMALS* series, visit our website at: ltta.tripod.com (no www, please). You can e-mail your story to: ltta@netreach.net, or mail it to LTTA, Box 214, East Greenville, PA 18041.

Some of the stories in this book came from Guideposts readers, just like you, and we welcome your participation in this inspiring series.

A Note From the Editors

---

*T*his original Guideposts series was created by the Book and Inspirational Media Division of the company that publishes *Guideposts,* a monthly magazine filled with true stories of people's adventures in faith.

Guideposts is available by subscription. All you have to do is write to Guideposts, 39 Seminary Hill Road, Carmel, New York 10512. When you subscribe, each month you can count on receiving exciting new evidence of God's presence, His guidance and His limitless love for all of us.

Guideposts Books are available on the World Wide Web at www.guidepostsbooks.com. Follow our popular book of devotionals, *Daily Guideposts,* and read excerpts from some of our best-selling books. You can also send prayer requests to our Monday morning Prayer Fellowship and read stories from recent issues of our magazines, *Guideposts, Angels on Earth,* and *Guideposts for Teens.*